Between / Beyond / Hybrid

Between / Beyond / Hybrid

New Essays on Transdisciplinarity

Edited by
Hartmut von Sass

DIAPHANES

Table of Contents

In Memoriam
Thomas Hengartner (1960–2018)

Preface

The Collegium Helveticum is Switzerland's only institute for advanced studies, run jointly by the Swiss Federal Institute of Technology (ETH), the University of Zurich, and the Zurich University of the Arts. This is a unique framework in which, for each four-year research period, scholars and artists from highly divergent backgrounds create projects and collaborations otherwise academically homeless, utopian, or at least unlikely.

In 2016 the Collegium gained a new director, the anthropologist and cultural scholar Thomas Hengartner who had previously been a professor of anthropology at the University of Zurich's Department of Social Anthropology and Cultural Studies. The papers collected here are based on contributions given at a 2016 international conference in Zurich celebrating the new transdisciplinary research period on "digital societies," which had just started as well as Thomas's incipient directorship.

The plan was to make these papers accessible to a wider audience by publishing them together, with him as co-editor. Things developed differently. Thomas Hengartner's untimely death in May 2018 turns this volume into a commemoration of him, but, more to the point, of the academic values and virtues he represented vividly: openness linked with a critical voice, curiosity combined with a particular interest, and crossing academic borders without losing disciplinary roots. May this volume participate in this threefold endeavor.

Hartmut von Sass, Zurich

Hartmut von Sass

Transdisciplinarity—a Drug on the Market?

An Introductory Question

The rhetoric of transdisciplinarity

The situation is rather ambivalent: on the one hand, the discourse on transdisciplinarity may already have adopted the status of a jargon, meaning that it is a crucial ingredient of the highly specific prose of submitting scientific proposals to endowments or public funding; on the other hand, and connected to the former point, "transdisciplinarity has lost its scientific glamour," as Sabine Maasen states in her paper, by being used in an inflationary manner and therefore in losing its grip and its semblance of evidence. This evidence was and is derived from the growing insight during the 1970s and 80s that a single subject is hardly able to deal with crucial challenges, social ones but also genuinely scientific problems. Hence, and speaking critically, transdisciplinarity serves as a response to the often enough vividly experienced impossibility of remaining a methodological solipsist. So transdisciplinary research counteracts the inclination to stick to one's own circle, and it pushes the scientist (and others) to risk crossing the boundaries of one's own field. To a large extent the more recent history of science is identical with the story of developing and organizing scientific collaborations between scientific disciplines, as well as with stakeholders from beyond the university. Nowadays, taking Switzerland as a representative example, transdisciplinarity is not a void confession but has already been integrated (since 1985) into Swiss research law. So it has achieved a constitutional level.[1]

Of course there is also a flipside to this, to which I have already alluded. The more transdisciplinarity is celebrated as an adequate response to current questions, the more it turns into a catchy keyword, and the more that happens without being counterbalanced by restricting its semantic scope—and who could be in charge of that?—the more "transdisciplinarity" loses its focus and meaning. So we could make a case here for the general claim that using a term in a fruitful manner also has to give an account of its limits. Transdisciplinarity, to clarify the point by exaggeration, might be suffering from its own early success. In this sense it could be regarded as "a drug on the market," in the ambiguous meaning of having inspired our thinking about science and influenced its institutional setting while having dominated the respective discourse for quite some time, so that the political rhetoric now needs a fresh new concept that will sell better in the decade to come.

However, these are only the more extreme alternatives, which neglect the nuances and space-in-between where the call for and the concept of transdisciplinarity is currently situated. Hence a more careful—and realistic—approach to transdisciplinarity has come to the fore, and it circles around the following questions:

—To what kind(s) of problems does transdisciplinarity as a programmatic account react, and is it a "reaction" to particular dynamics in the first place?

1 See René Bloch, "Inter- und Transdiziplinarität im schweizerischen Hochschulbereich," in Frédéric Darbellay and Theres Paulsen (eds.), *Herausforderung Inter- und Transdiziplinarität. Konzepte, Methoden und innovative Umsetzung in Lehre und Forschung*, Lausanne: EPFL Press, 2008, p. 292.

—Is the call for transdisciplinarity more than a political attempt to meet what have been called "the grand challenges," and if so, in which sense precisely?

—How to relate the necessary collaboration between disciplines as well as non-scientific actors with a strong notion of disciplinarity?

—Is transdisciplinarity really a new development within science and its environment or is it rather an integral part of particular disciplines? (Or is this an unhappy alternative?)

—Is transdisciplinarity primarily a structural and therefore an institutional approach to upheavals in the architecture of scientific projects, or is it also, as René Bloch suggests, a human desire to communicate, even something "voyeuristic,"[2] to see what others are doing beyond one's own fence? (Perhaps these are, again, insufficient options.)

—What concrete status does transdisciplinarity enjoy: is it a way of organizing scientific endeavors, or is it a set of rules and methods?

Thinking about transdisciplinarity means thinking about these questions. In this introductory note the focus is not on answering them but rather on deepening our understanding of them.

The discipline within transdisciplinarity

Discipline—again an (intentionally) ambivalent term. On the one hand transdisciplinarity sets high standards and demands on those working successfully on that basis; and on the other hand the call for transdisciplinary research makes the question of how we deal with the traditional subjects and disciplines, and

2 Ibid., p. 298.

how we should combine being anchored in one field with collaborations beyond these limits, rather urgent.

Let us begin with the first dimension of this twofold concept. In this regard transdisciplinarity (not sharply distinguished so far from inter- or multidisciplinarity) goes hand in hand with a certain kind of scientific attitude and ethos. Even within a single discipline one is called to be open to other voices, to fruitful irritation by other ideas, constructive contradiction and critique. This is not only amplified by transdisciplinarity, however; other elements that are not relevant within one subject are of additional importance here. It is what Maasen calls "interactional expertise," i.e. the willingness to translate one's own concepts for scientific foreigners and to remain open to their language games following other, partly alien rules. Since there is no scientific "Esperanto" the readiness to translate, rephrase, and find fitting examples—as well as the openness to understand the other person, combined with the stubbornness to ask for another explanation—a different circumscription is essential. This serious game of giving and receiving reasons, explanations, and examples constitutes the "trading zone" between different disciplinary subjects, programs, and orientations. In this first sense, transdisciplinarity then stands for or entails a *scientific virtue* (or a set of them) that faces the fact of differences in values and vocabularies and acknowledges these demarcations in a fruitful way. Again Maasen coined the fitting term "informed dissent" for this constellation.

Apart from transdisciplinary discipline as attitude or virtue, transdisciplinarity sheds new light on what it was initially introduced to counterbalance (not to overcome), namely the mere disciplinary focus. Put in question form: What is the outlook of the traditional disciplines in a transdisciplinary era? Is transdisciplinary research increasingly substituting the old canon of separated subjects, or are both scientific orientations, disciplinary and transdisciplinary, compatible? There are at least three ways to answer this question. First, it is true that there is a *dynamic of replacement* in acknowledging the fact that a single field can hardly deal with the issues at hand, and then in approaching problems in a transdisciplinary manner. Cybernetics might serve as an older but influential example burdened, back in the 1940s and 50s, with high hopes of being a new all-encompassing meta-theory;[3] a related, more recent example is cognitive science as a collaboration between natural and social sciences and the humanities. Second, we have seen developments within transdisciplinary research, for instance between chemistry, physics, and biology, that resulted in the institutionalization of a new discipline, in this case biochemistry. So inter-subject effort created a new one, and transdisciplinarity turned into an *updated version of disciplinarity*. Third, one can defend, as Jürgen Mittelstrass does, that true *transdisciplinarity presupposes a strong disciplinary background*.[4] The "trans" only makes sense if there is something to transgress; a collaboration is only possible when there actually are initially separate players. This is just a logical and rather trivial point, but we are also dealing here with practical implications in regard to the educational setting in universities. Yet the current shift from departments and faculties based on a disciplinary structure to centers and institutes for advanced studies promoting a trans- or interdisciplinary context is only fruitful if this shift creates an additional potential instead of substituting the system that is the condition of transdisciplinarity.

These three developments—replacement, updating, presupposition—should not rule each other out, but rather go hand in hand and represent parallel dynamics interacting in various ways. Then we could expect the discipline within trans-

3 See W. Ross Ashby, *An Introduction to Cybernetics*, London: Chapman & Hall, 1957, chapter 1.

4 See Jürgen Mittelstrass's paper in this issue; see also Jürgen Mittelstrass, *Die unzeitgemässe Universität*, Frankfurt am Main: Suhrkamp, 1994, pp. 108–110.

disciplinary research to enrich the faculties of scientific work by successfully broadening the ways in which science is conducted.

Transdisciplinarity as a scientific concept

There are two basic understandings of the range of collaborations described as transdisciplinary. According to the wider version, transdisciplinarity encompasses scientific and non-scientific collaborators, and opens up the concept to art, stakeholders, companies, etc. Here transdisciplinary work is usually more focussed on concrete practical problems solely or better solvable by this kind of *transscientific* joint venture. The narrower understanding of transdisciplinarity, however, speaks of a genuinely scientific concept without regard to fields outside academia.

Let us briefly focus on this second version, which again allows for two different readings. The first might be called *structural*, where transdisciplinarity is a process in which different subjects successively find a way of working together; the second could be called *natural*, meaning that the transdisciplinary element is already an integral part of a discipline or a subject.

Structural transdisciplinarity is the common version, and, historically speaking, it precedes the "naturally" transdisciplinary subjects. During the 1970s—the high time of interdisciplinarity—it served as a response to the technological consequences of modernization. In this sense, inter- and later transdisciplinarity also implied an element of compensating for the pitfalls and insufficiencies within the traditional architecture of scientific subjects. This new structure was then also institutionalized. In Germany, the first explicitly interdisciplinary institute, the ZiF in Bielefeld, was founded in 1968; other similar institutions were supposed to follow.

The increasing significance and acceptance of institutionalized collaborations also called for conceptual differentiations between *multi*disciplinarity (a shared focus on one project without necessarily unifying methods), *inter*disciplinarity (a temporary project to which different scientific disciplines contribute), and *trans*disciplinarity (as a permanent research principle for collaboration between scientific disciplines and, potentially, beyond). These three concepts are not sharply distinguished, and they have overlapping elements; despite some significant differences, these labels could also be applied heuristically, apart from the fact that—as we have already seen—they do not amount to one thing and are often enough used differently. We could furthermore ponder on the possibility of whether multi-, inter-, and transdisciplinarity merge into one another, or whether there is an internal hierarchy between them.

Let us now turn to the "natural" version. Contrary to its structural counterpart, "natural" transdisciplinarity is not a development or dynamic between different disciplines amounting to a collaborative endeavor, but is rather an essential feature of a single discipline. Transdisciplinarity did not only change the structure of subjects and disciplines; there are subjects and disciplines that are intrinsically transdisciplinary. This is why the somewhat tendentious term "natural" was coined to express this kind of inner-disciplinary ramification. In her paper, Andrea Braidt highlights this kind of transdisciplinarity within one discipline in reference to media and gender studies, which did not develop into a transdisciplinary direction but had been founded from the start as transdisciplinary disciplines. But the question remains as to the extent to which this "natural" transdisciplinarity entails a given set of defining theories and methods. Braidt expresses her doubts that this is the case, but leaves room for that possibility, surely dependent on the specific field in question.

Transdisciplinarity—going beyond science

Up to this point we have stayed within the border—and perhaps also within the limits—of genuinely *scientific* research. According to this view, transdisciplinarity denotes a particular collaboration between different subjects. One might raise the further question as to whether this understanding entails additional presuppositions about shared methods and goals. However, essential for this version—again, put forward and defended by Jürgen Mittelstrass[5]—is the *scientific* character of transdisciplinary research.[6] This changes as soon as we extend the scope of "transdisciplinarity." According to this extended version, we have to recognize that transdisciplinary practices not only include the knowledge of different scientific disciplines but also of extra-scientific approaches from arts, economic stake-holders, start-ups, and so on, as well as the negotiation of knowledge in the public sphere.

There is a second difference to the traditional view, namely that not only does transdisciplinarity integrate non- or extra-scientific forms of expertise, but also that the goal—the *telos*—of transdisciplinary endeavors has changed. This refers to the solution (or a contribution) to a socially relevant problem, such as the "grand challenges" of environment and climate change,

5 See Jürgen Mittelstrass, "Methodische Transdisziplinarität," in *Technikfolgenabschätzung: Theorie und Praxis*, 14:2 (2005), pp. 18–23.

6 See also the related definition of transdisciplinarity by Antonius Liedhegener (et. al.): transdisciplinarity can "be understood as shared research undertaken by different disciplines, oriented to problems relevant to the individual disciplines, with the aim of a scientifically more precise identification of social problems, their analysis, and if possible the generation of knowledge about solutions and applications"; translated from Antonius Liedhegener and Andreas Tunger-Zanetti, "Religion, Wirtschaft, Politik transdisziplinär – eine Herausforderung," in Antonius Liedhegener, Andreas Tunger-Zanetti and Stephan Wirz (eds.), *Religion – Wirtschaft – Politik: Forschungszugänge zu einem aktuellen transdisziplinären Feld*, Baden-Baden / Zurich: Pano / Nomos, 2011, p. 17.

famine and poverty, health and aging, digitalization, etc. Transdisciplinarity then amounts to pushing the borders set by the university, and it derives its name from a dynamic leading away from simply scientific concerns, but also from purely interdisciplinary collaboration by stressing various forms of knowledge. Transdisciplinarity would thus not primarily be a collaboration of disciplines, since it would not bring together representatives of various subjects but of different intellectual, social, political, and artistic commitments. The "trans" in transdisciplinarity not only alters the way interdisciplinarity works; it also entails another picture of collaborations within and beyond the scientific demarcation line.

This is one reason why the arts have gained more attention from the sciences lately, either through their integration—as a certain kind of knowledge—into a scientific canon (not always welcomed by the arts themselves) or through an appreciation of their own voice and approach to "epistemic things," in the sense highlighted by Hans-Jörg Rheinberger.[7] The question arises more vividly here as to whether the "things" dealt with in a transdisciplinary manner are already "out there," or whether they are the emerging products of a collaboration at the boundaries of disciplines, subjects, and approaches that play with these borders in a seriously productive way.

Transdisciplinary research: structural implications

We have distinguished between transdisciplinarity as an innerscientific collaboration on the one hand—in this sense we can follow Jürgen Mittelstrass in saying that transdisciplinarity is

7 See Hans-Jörg Rheinberger, *Toward a History of Epistemic Things: Synthesizing Proteins in the Test Tube*, Redwood City, CA: Stanford University Press, 1997, pp. 24–37.

nothing but successful interdisciplinarity[8]— and on the other, transdisciplinarity as a collaborative mode of integrating agents beyond science, such as artists, politicians, companies, etc.[9] Both versions, especially the second one, change the scientific landscape in at least two crucial and sustainable ways. They call for other capacities—openness, translation, understanding—and require new structures to enable successful work beyond the traditional frameworks.

We have already touched on the quest for the "transdisciplinary type" as someone who is able to deal with the Babylon-like experience of different languages. Accordingly, the challenges and hindrances to transdisciplinary work are described as semantic barriers. Either you have to find a common language or you set up a framework for mutual understanding. But of course there are also divergent approaches to scientific work—methods, goals, expectations—that lead beyond the "trading zones" for finding a common language and construct "boundary objects," which serve as general reference while being open to different interpretations.[10] Both the finding of a shared language as well as the establishment of these open objects are elements of scientific negotiation or even diplomacy.

These protagonists all have to go through a system that had and still has to change considerably in regard to transdisciplinary demands. The traditional university structure—since the days of Humboldt and Schleiermacher—has been based on faculties that mirror the focus on different subjects and disciplines. The post-traditional university structure, however, has to adopt new forms of self-organization to enable fruitful

8 See Jürgen Mittelstrass, "On Transdisciplinarity," in *Trames: A Journal of the Humanities and Social Sciences* 15:4 (2011), pp. 329–338.

9 See Florian Dombois's paper in this publication.

10 See Helga Nowotny, Peter Scott, Michael Gibbons, *Re-Thinking Science: Knowledge and the Public in an Age of Uncertainty*, Cambridge: Polity, 2001, pp. 3–165.

transdisciplinarity. As a consequence, many universities have ceased to organize their departments and study programs solely in disciplines, but do so according to other parameters, such as dimensions, common goals, tasks, or topics. Faculties are being accompanied and partly even replaced by other structures beyond faculties and departments. This goes for traditional universities, but even more for art schools. Here, rather than being transdisciplinary, the tendency often proposes a *non*disciplinary perspective. In this context, transdisciplinarity does not primarily work as a scientific principle (or even a method), but rather as an agenda for organizing the university of the future.[11] And for this future it is often enough still an open question how to relate the traditional disciplinary structure to transdisciplinary requirements, in terms of the political architecture for our universities as well as their institutional structures in teaching and degrees.

Transdisciplinarity and its limits

Every branch has its waves of excitement about new developments lingering over new trends and promises. And these waves are usually followed by a period of calming down, sometimes even of disenchantment and eventually a more realistic and balanced attitude. Both the initial excitement and the slight disillusionment can be fruitful in leading to a more nuanced progress. One could make the case that transdisciplinarity as a programmatic paradigm played—and is partly still playing—a similar role in science research. It might serve to articulate the hope (or even expectation) of solving urgent problems and leading necessarily beyond the old and outmoded limits of separated fields,

11 See also Harald Atmanspacher's reply to Jürgen Mittelstrass in this publication.

subjects, and methods. However, we have already entered the period *after* the excitement, when the pros and cons of this paradigm are more graspable or are being allowed to emerge.

The early arousal might have been caused, as Harald Atmanspacher suggests,[12] by simply being novel at the time these transdisciplinary approaches were established. They could thus provide the opportunity to work with flexible boundaries between interrelated subunits, and hence support the interest-driven discourse between excellent individual researchers. Nevertheless, all this might have been just an initial transient phase that was in danger of decay and vanishing as soon as structures began to stabilize as they developed into more institutionalized frameworks or as we got accustomed to the new language games of an unknown paradigm. But as we all know, the new necessarily turns into the old at some point, and then this discourse will call for a new wave, another excitement, the next paradigm.

These temporal issues are based on general observations concerning the dynamics of discourses not solely typical for scientific trends. However, one can also point to internal difficulties connected to transdisciplinary research—and I would like to name three aspects: First, transdisciplinarity presupposes a disciplinary anchor and discipline-based education. We cannot work together as long as this back-up does not exist; it is still the case that disciplines are at the center of every university's architecture—and it is safe to predict that this general structure will prevail. This does not need to be an expression of educational conservatism, but it might be a reflection of requiring disciplinary experts to make a success of transdisciplinary projects. In this sense, transdisciplinarity does not substitute the disciplinary base but might even strengthen it.

Second, and this is a point underlined in Andrea Braidt's paper, obviously not every problem calls for a transdisciplinary

12 See ibid.

solution. Most of the scientific challenges are answerable by traditional disciplinary tools. Hence the idea that transdisciplinarity serves as a *sine qua non* for academic thinking does not make much sense. It covers a part of the solutions sciences are looking for, but a part does not imply the whole. We may accordingly assume that another collaboration emerges here, one between transdisciplinary and traditional orientations in sciences (and beyond).

Third, transdisciplinarity has always elicited the precarious question of how to do it. Attempts to meet this question lead to another one, which we touched on above, namely whether transdisciplinarity is a set of explicit methods or a way of organizing scientific endeavors (or both). How to do it looks very different if we consider transdisciplinarity to be a method or an issue of structuring (or institutionalizing) research. If we go with the *methodological* reading, we will at some point come across the difficulty of going beyond circumscriptions of transdisciplinary work (see above, scientific virtues) without being able to exactly pin down a set of identifiable methods. It seems doubtful that they really exist. If we go with the *structural* reading, we could refer to the vast amount of institutions intending to be locations of transdisciplinarity. But they differ too greatly in their structures to truly secure transdisciplinary research and to sustainably avoid the usual falling back into one's own scientific home. But here again it is not easy to indicate the particular rules to follow in order to identify the conditions for transdisciplinary success—which is itself a non-evident notion.

Outlook: on this publication

The contributions in this publication go back to papers given at the Collegium Helveticum in Zurich during the fall semester 2016. Most of them are based on presentations to a conference on transdisciplinarity that took place at the Collegium in

November of that year. Some of the important and prominent voices that shaped the discourse on transdisciplinarity within the German-speaking scene contribute here as well; all of the authors involved here have to do, practically and scientifically, with the treasures and pitfalls of transdisciplinary research.

This is the first sense in which this publication is itself a transdisciplinary expression. In a second sense it is true because all authors come from very different areas on the scientific landscape, and insofar as exchange and discussion at a conference on transdisciplinary research is itself part of their subject matter, then this publication truly goes beyond the disciplines. A third aspect is the involvement of the arts—see the papers by Florian Dombois, Marco Meier, and, more indirectly, Andrea Braidt—which concerns the broader version of transdisciplinarity leaving the defined limits of the academic realm. An additional and fourth aspect lies in the fact that all main papers are followed by short responses presented by scholars coming from an intentionally different subject and background. Fifth and last, the location: the Collegium Helveticum as the host institute regards itself as a transdisciplinary laboratory, a fact that turns this debate—in a time after the excitement that initially infused transdisciplinarity as a programmatic endeavor—into a critical self-reflection on the structures, intentions, and possible failure of current projects, as well as our understanding of their potential success.

Jürgen Mittelstrass

From Disciplinarity and Interdisciplinarity to Trans-disciplinarity and Back Again

Preliminary Remarks

For centuries, the order of knowledge seemed to be taken for granted, almost as something natural, especially when we think of the way research and teaching at universities is structured. This structure was given by an order of disciplines, structured in subjects, which followed their own respective theoretical and methodological standards. Interdisciplinarity, as part of this structure, was accordingly the dialogue between disciplines, sometimes less and sometimes more intense, but always conducted from the safe viewpoint of the respective disciplines. Examples of this are a *studium generale,* which used to be mandatory, and lecture series between disciplines, which were from the beginning defined as non-mandatory.

This has since changed. Interdisciplinarity has suddenly become widely discussed. Academia preaches it where program reform is concerned, and science[1] in particular when advertis-

1 I use here and in the following the term "science" in a broad sense, according to the German term "Wissenschaft," i.e. including the humanities and arts. A different version with the title "The Order of Knowledge: From Disciplinarity to Interdisciplinarity and Back" has been published in the *European Review: Interdisciplinary Journal of the Academia Europea* 26, suppl. 52 (Crossing over to the Future: Interdisciplinarity in Research and Higher Education) (2018), pp. 1–8.

ing its research. But even so, this does not yet seem satisfying. The further concept of transdisciplinarity is being introduced and is usually used to counteract the old-fashioned, non-binding nature of the concept of interdisciplinarity by the idea of a binding form of cooperation that is almost enforced by the development of science itself. In transdisciplinarity, the disciplines lose their formerly dominant role. Those who want to show their inclusiveness in science speak of interdisciplinarity, and those who want to show that they are at the methodological forefront speak of transdisciplinarity. Even within science policy, transdisciplinarity is used when trying to give an impression of theoretical sophistication. It often appears that what is meant by what is now called transdisciplinarity is as self-evident as interdisciplinarity. However, this is not true when we take a closer look. While there are attempts to define transdisciplinarity as an elaborated methodology and to recommend it to the sciences, this rests more on a misunderstanding than an insight, i.e., the misunderstanding that transdisciplinarity is something which can be formulated in theoretical, here methodological, form. I will come back to this later.

The question is, in any case, how what is now called transdisciplinarity, in contrast to the common interdisciplinarity, is related to the disciplinary structure of science and the respective problems of science, as well as to the problems caused by general technical and social development. One might also ask how transdisciplinarity, in contrast to the common disciplines and interdisciplinarity, helps us to advance in the sciences and in the world in which we live and work.

Disciplinarity and interdisciplinarity

The sciences are organized by subjects and disciplines. Geometry is a subject in the discipline of mathematics, and English studies is a subject in the disciplines of literature and linguistics. Those who teach at university teach a subject within a discipline, and whoever attends a university studies a subject within a discipline. So far, everything seems in order. There is a firm scientific architecture, which is expressed institutionally in the form of institutes (colleges, schools) and departments or faculties (discipline structure). This is what I call the *epistemic* and the *organizational structure* of science. The one, the epistemic structure, concerns the order of knowledge, while the other, the organizational structure, concerns the institutional order of subjects and disciplines within the university. What is interdisciplinarity in this context, and why is it so important?

Interdisciplinarity, strange as this may at first sound given its current popularity, is really an ancient idea of science. However, it presented itself in a very different way from today, and concerned the fact that the knowledge of various disciplines was closely linked, that the path into one discipline also led into other disciplines, that specialists did not yet exist, and that science was philosophy and philosophy was science. However, it was particular individuals who held all the knowledge together, even in the disciplinary forms that were emerging; its structure was not dictated by a scholarly architecture. The unity of science, which is still occasionally talked about, was less of an idea—which it was to become later—than simply reality.

In Aristotle—let us remain for a moment at the beginning—this is illustrated most impressively. While the Pre-Socratics were still primarily thinking about becoming and passing away, which were later appropriated by physics and biology, and Plato analyzed the knowledge of his time under epistemic and pedagogical aspects, Aristotle designed a research program that covered the entire cosmos of knowledge; or better, he created it. This knowledge ranges from logic to physics, from astronomy to biology, from metaphysics to ethics, from psychology to political science, and so on. Only mathematics failed to gain any significant, new insight from Aristotle. What could interdisciplinarity as a special form of scientific knowledge mean here?

What comes from a single mind or is held together by a single mind does not require any elaborate bridges between different areas of knowledge, even if it is precisely the Aristotelian work that forms the basis of the emerging disciplinary structure. Gilbert Ryle, one of the great modern philosophers, concludes his take on the Aristotelian achievement with the following words: "The university has come into existence."[2] At most Leibniz or Kant's work were later to reach this level of universality.

In this sense interdisciplinarity, understood simply as a path between the disciplines, neither has its own epistemic and organizational status, nor does it support further scientific development—for example, as a particular form of competence. Rather, it turns out to be a kind of competence to unite where disciplinary knowledge goes its own way and separates itself from other disciplinary knowledge, where it develops diversity in the form of intradisciplinary special forms, and where Aristotelian universality is missing.

Now it would be profoundly unrealistic to think we would only have to find universal thinkers such as Aristotle again for interdisciplinarity to return to being unremarkable. The cosmos of scientific knowledge has expanded too much and has become too diverse. Moreover, science is not only about answering one's own questions and solving one's own problems with the appropriate disciplinary means; it is also more and more about helping to answer questions and to solve problems outside the inner world of science; that is, in ordinary life, both in the natural and in the social realms. The scientific world is not a closed world, for which the well-known metaphor of the ivory tower stands, but—whether science likes it or not—an open one.

2 G. Ryle, "Plato," in P. Edwards (ed.), *The Encyclopedia of Philosophy*, vols. 1–8, New York and London: Macmillan, 1967, vol. 6, p. 333.

This is true not only in organizational or institutional respects, but also in epistemic respects: at least in the sense that it is not always possible to sharply distinguish answering questions and giving solutions to problems as scientific questions, and problems which concern science at its core, from answering such questions and giving solutions which concern the world. Nuclear research, in the form of fusion research, for example, is not pursued for its own sake, which is only interesting to the researcher, but also for solving our energy problems, which is of interest to us all. The same applies to medical and climate research. Here too it is not so much a matter of solving problems which are inner-scientific, and thereby "invented" by the scientific community, but rather a matter of solving the most problematic health and environmental problems.

That science is increasingly divided into professional and disciplinary specializations is also unsurprising. This fact is not a result of an unwanted development, which would have to be corrected by means of interdisciplinary measures, but by progress in science. Development into subjects and disciplines is here the consequence of scientific success, which is often not in the core area of a subject or discipline where textbook knowledge is located, but rather in peripheral areas that can be closer to subjects and disciplines other than one's own. This is true in both substantial and theoretical or methodological respects. Neither the subjects of research nor the theories and methods used in research are generally mutually exclusive or disciplinary. The same objects, e.g. plant structures, can be the interest of different subjects and disciplines. The same theories, e.g., mathematical theories, and the same methods, e.g., empirical methods, can prove fruitful across many subjects and disciplines. Moreover, specialization does not only have to take place within a discipline, it also often takes place between subjects or disciplines. "Nano" could be a keyword here. Interdisciplinarity, in turn, is expected to reconcile the different epistemic and organizational or institutional structures. But is that enough?

Transdisciplinarity

Given the developments described above, the scientific system has become alarmingly complex.[3] This is true not only with regard to the tremendous growth of knowledge, which is impossible to follow in all details even within the narrower context of a subject, but in respect of the institutional structure of science. The specialization of subjects reaches even into the naming of chairs. The ability to think within a larger scientific unit, such as a discipline, let alone to think beyond one, is decreasing alarmingly. But this means that the boundaries of subjects and of disciplines, if still correctly perceived at all, are increasingly threatened to become not only institutional boundaries, but also the limits of knowledge.

Here we should remember that the subjects and disciplines of science are nothing "natural" or "God-given," but something that came about from the history of science, and that their boundaries are often not theoretical, i.e., systematically determined, but rather historical. Their scientific-historical identity is also defined by certain research subjects, theories, methods, and research purposes, which often do not together form a specialization or discipline—as I have already mentioned—but interfere at an interdisciplinary level. This is illustrated not only by the fact that disciplines in their work are guided by methodological and theoretical ideas, which they themselves could not produce independently, but also by the fact that problems, and thus their solutions, can change the framework of their discipline or subject. A good example of this is the theoretical description of heat. Heat was regarded first as the inner move-

3 See J. Mittelstrass, "Interdisziplinarität oder Transdisziplinarität?" in L. Hieber (ed.), *Utopie Wissenschaft. Ein Symposium an der Universität Hannover über die Chancen des Wissenschaftsbetriebs der Zukunft (21./22. November 1991)*, Munich and Vienna: Profil, 1993, pp. 17–31; also in J. Mittelstrass, *Die Häuser des Wissens: Wissenschaftstheoretische Studien*, Frankfurt am Main: Suhrkamp, 1998, pp. 29–48.

ment of matter and thus as the object of physics. With the caloric theory, developed by the Dutch physician and scientist Boerhaave at the beginning of the eighteenth century and further developed by the French chemist Lavoisier, heat, because it was now understood as being matter, then became the object of the study of chemistry. Finally, with the kinetic theory of heat, it again changed disciplines to return to being an object of physics. This further shows that it is not the objects of research (alone) that define the discipline, but the way in which we deal with them theoretically. This is clear for research, but often not for a discipline's self-image.

This example can be generalized and at the same time applied to the wider world, i.e., not only to scientifically defined problems, in such a way that certain problems escape the access of a single subject or discipline. And these are often by no means marginal problems, such as those concerning the environment, energy, and health. There is an asymmetry regarding the development of problems and disciplines (or subjects), and this is exacerbated by the fact that developments in disciplines and subjects are determined by growing specialization. Ecological problems, for instance, are complex problems; as we all now know, they can only be solved by the cooperation of the competences of many subjects and disciplines, which are usually specialized competences. The same is true of energy and health, as well as many other areas that cannot make progress without science. If, therefore, the problems do not do us the favor of defining themselves as disciplinary or as falling under one subject, then we also need special efforts that usually lead us away from subjects or disciplines. This is precisely what the term "interdisciplinarity" has so far been used for, and it is exactly what the term "transdisciplinarity" is used for today. This is not just a semantic change, however.

While scientific cooperation in the form of interdisciplinarity usually means temporary cooperation, transdisciplinarity means that cooperation leads to a permanent scientific order that changes the structure of the subjects and disciplines. Transdisciplinarity is presented as *a form of carrying out research*, thus as a form of science when it concerns problems of the common world, e.g., to solve the environmental, energy, and health problems mentioned above, and also when it concerns the order of scientific knowledge and scientific research itself. In both cases, transdisciplinarity is *a research* or *science principle*, and not a *theory principle*. It is relevant where the definition of a problem or the solution to a problem within a subject or discipline is not possible, or where the definition of problems or solutions lead beyond subjects or disciplines.[4]

Pure forms of transdisciplinarity appear no more than the pure form of disciplinarity. That too is usually understood and realized in the context of neighboring scientific approaches, for example with sociological aspects in the work of the historian, philosophical aspects in the work of the legal scholar, or chemical aspects in the work of the biologist. To this extent, disciplinarity and transdisciplinarity are research-guiding principles or ideal forms of scientific research, while mixed forms are the norm. It is important only that science and research are conscious of this, and that productive research is not limited by technical and disciplinary restrictions that are outdated (and usually habitual). Such a limitation serves neither scientific progress nor a world which, in view of its own problems, wishes to admire science less than use it.

In other words, transdisciplinarity, as portrayed here in contrast to interdisciplinarity, is firstly an *integrative* concept. It eliminates isolation that has emerged in scientific practice, and can often only be explained historically, at a higher method-

4 For different views on the concept of transdisciplinarity and related problems see G. Hirsch Hadorn et al. (eds.), *Handbook of Transdisciplinary Research*, New York: Springer, 2007; J. T. Klein, "Evaluation of Interdisciplinary and Transdisciplinary Research," in *American Journal of Preventive Medicine* 35, Supplement (2008), pp. 116–123.

ological level, but it does not pursue a universal interpretation and explanation pattern. Secondly, transdisciplinarity eliminates shortcomings that evolved over time where subjects and disciplines have lost their historical memory and problem-solving power because of too much specialization. But transdisciplinarity does not lead to a new subject or discipline, and therefore it cannot replace them. Thirdly, transdisciplinarity is a research and organizational principle that, in being problem-oriented, goes beyond subjects and disciplines. But it is not a trans-scientific principle that goes beyond science. Transdisciplinarity is a scientific view, and it is directed at a world that is a scientific and technical entity, being more and more the work of scientific and technical reason. Finally and fourthly, transdisciplinarity, as I have mentioned already, is first and foremost a research principle, not a theory principle. It is at most secondarily a theory principle, if the theories also follow a transdisciplinary research program. Depending on whether a solution is a solution to an inner-scientific problem, i.e., a problem formulated by science itself, or a problem given by the world, I would like to speak of *theoretical* and *practical* transdisciplinarity, both of which can go hand in hand, where theoretical transdisciplinarity can also serve practical transdisciplinarity.

Examples

An example of theoretical transdisciplinarity is *structural research*, i.e., the development, analysis, manipulation, and ultimately the practical application (in this case the theoretical becomes the practical transdisciplinarity) of structures of a certain order of magnitude, equally interesting for physics, chemistry, and biology, but also for geology and material and computer science. The idea of exploring and designing functional structures to the order of magnitude between 10–9 and 10–6 meters, i.e., single atoms, molecules, and small accumulations of atoms, goes back to a visionary talk that physicist and later Nobel laureate Richard P. Feynman gave at a meeting of the American Physical Society (APS) at the California Institute of Technology in Pasadena in 1959.[5] In this talk Feynman dealt among other things with the storage and reading of information in a very small space, thus anticipating a series of lithographic methods currently in use.

Feynman, as he himself writes, was inspired by biology, in which such small and highly functional structures are actually found. Why then should not it be possible to produce them artificially? Nanotechnologists investigate extremely small (mostly biological) functional structures in nature, e.g., membranes, enzymes, and other cellular components, and further seek to create these structures in experiments with the aid of semiconductors, for example, and to simulate their properties using a computer. In such a production of nanostructures, physicists and chemists work hand in hand. While physicists usually begin with a given structure, such as a surface, on which they then work using physical methods, chemists begin at the level of atoms and molecules in order to put them together in a systematic way. All areas of nanotechnological research are closely linked; advances in one area usually bring about progress in others.

An example of practical transdisciplinarity, which crucially presupposes theoretical transdisciplinarity, is *climate research*. This makes it particularly clear how different competencies of subjects and disciplines must interrelate in order to deal with the tremendous complexity of climate and its causes and transformations, and the corresponding consequences for life on earth. This is about understanding the global cycles of water, carbon, nitrogen, and other elements that determine climate

5 R. Feynman, "There's Plenty of Room at the Bottom," in *Engineering and Science* 23 (1960), pp. 22–36.

that are not purely natural, but also influenced by humans, e.g., by the emission of greenhouse gases. It is moreover about chemical processes such as ozone depletion in the stratosphere and the increase of ozone in the troposphere, as well as changes caused by irregularities in the earth's orbit around the sun and changes in the physical and chemical structure of the earth itself. Continuing population growth and increasing industrialization and urbanization are doing their utmost to make research into the earth and especially its climate system an ongoing challenge.

With simulations and model calculations, i.e., scenarios involving idealized emission and concentration assumptions, climate research is trying to tackle this complexity (with an eye to prediction), which is influenced by fluctuating and feedback effects, with moderate and controversial success. After all, evidence suggests global warming by 0.2° C in the coming decade, even by 0.1° C, if the concentration of all greenhouse gases and aerosols, i.e., invisible particles suspended in the air that have an influence on the heat balance given their particular chemical composition, are kept constant at roughly their level over the last few years.

A classic example of the fundamental difficulties encountered in the area of climate prediction is the so-called *ozone hole* or the effect of chlorofluorocarbon on the ozone layer of the higher atmosphere. The interaction of chemical reactions is so complex that this effect could hardly have been *predicted*; it was difficult enough to *explain* it after it had been discovered. It is just as common that small causes often have great effects that are hardly predictable. Thus glacial periods, according to current knowledge, are ultimately based on a relatively slight cooling of the earth's atmosphere. This, in turn, is due to slightly reduced solar radiation that results from peculiarities of the earth's orbital motion around the sun, namely its varying eccentricity and the varying orientation and inclination of the earth's axis. The crucial point is that this slight cooling seems to lead to a change in the currents of the North Atlantic. In particular, a warm current is diverted that rises to the sea surface near Iceland and is responsible for the relatively mild winters of Europe. As a result, the winters in the northern hemisphere become considerably more severe and this, in turn, causes a worldwide cooling of considerable extent. Small changes in the peripheral conditions in this case cause a great change in the corresponding state of the system. The same applies to the so-called butterfly effect, i.e., the fact that slight changes in climatic conditions can lead to chaotic effects. Thus the reliability of climate prediction is not only limited in practice but also in principle. These occur, although the underlying laws are known and deterministic in nature.

It is no wonder that the common subject-related and disciplinary paths lead nowhere if pursued in isolation. This is also true for related technical innovations that often concern only the symptoms and not the causes, one such innovation being so-called *CCS technology* (*Carbon Capture & Storage*), which is intended to extract the CO_2 from power plants and to store it underground (and thereby uses about 50 percent of the energy produced). Accordingly, the Max Planck Society formulates as the most urgent tasks of geo- and climate research in general: (1) the "study of the spatial and temporal variations in the structure and composition of all earth systems, from the inner core to the upper atmosphere, through improved observation-, theory- and modeling-capacities"; (2) the "study of the connections between physical and chemical processes, with special consideration of the energy exchange within and between the components of the earth-sun system"; and (3) the "study of marine and terrestrial ecosystems and their evolution as well as the interactions of the biosphere with the processes of the 'system earth'." At the same time, the Max Planck Society refers to the need for an "integrated understanding" of the "connections and feedback effects between the various physical, chemical, geological, biological, and social systems of the earth, their development and effects on the metabolism and the bio-complexity of the planet earth."[6]

So much for these two examples. As to the distinction between theoretical and practical transdisciplinarity, which these examples were supposed to illustrate, the two actually go hand in hand as the climate example shows. In both cases the same methodological problems arise, especially when it involves an institutional order of subjects and disciplines. After all, any form of practical transdisciplinarity depends on theoretically gained knowledge, and not every combination of competences from various subjects or disciplines leads to success (which could easily be documented in the earlier forms of loosely handled interdisciplinarity). What is at stake? Here is another example, this time non-empirical but that takes empirical research into account.

In 2000 the Berlin-Brandenburg Academy of Sciences and Humanities set up a research group concerning the establishment of *health standards*, motivated by the peculiar fact that health is still a vague concept, both in the scientific world and in ordinary life, and is usually defined as the absence of disease (the lexicographic entry under "health" often says "see: sickness"), remaining oddly empty. Another motivation came from the dismal state of the German health system, which cannot be dealt with by typical patchwork solutions. Here, more fundamental considerations are required, and the necessary clarifications should reach deeper into anthropological and ethical considerations. The working group included physicians, lawyers, economists, biologists, historians, and philosophers. The results were presented in a study in 2004 titled *Gesundheit nach Maß?*[7]

6 http://www.mpg.de/forschungsgebiete/CPT/GEO/Geo_Klimaforschung/index.html.

7 C. F. Gethmann et al., *Gesundheit nach Maß? Eine transdisziplinäre Studie zu den Grundlagen eines dauerhaften Gesundheitssystems*, Berlin: Akademie Verlag, 2004.

What were the problems of such a group, and how were they solved in a methodologically identifiable way? The actual process was such that the disciplines, represented by different disciplinary competences, worked together, starting from drafts determined by the respective disciplines of the physician, the lawyer, the economist, and the philosopher, for example, which resulted, after repeated revisions under varying disciplinary aspects, in a collaborative outcome. The requirements for this (in a chronological order) were: (1) the unrestricted will to learn and the willingness to allow their disciplinary ideas to be scrutinized; (2) the development of transdisciplinary competence in a productive dialogue with other disciplinary approaches; (3) the ability to reformulate their own approaches in light of the transdisciplinary competence gained; (4) the production of a common text in which the unity of the argument ("transdisciplinary unity") replaces a mere aggregate of disciplinary parts. In this particular case these requirements were satisfied and the described process succeeded.

The methodologically reconstructable stages were, briefly: a disciplinary approach, the demoting of disciplinarity, the gaining of transdisciplinary competence, the purging of disciplinarity in the arguments, and transdisciplinarity as an argumentative unit. The crucial factor in this non-empirical investigation, but one that took empirical results into account, is its *argumentative nature*, i.e., the fact that the whole process, in a non-trivial sense, took place in the argumentative sphere. In our example the establishment of health standards or of measures for a healthy life was generated over different disciplines and simultaneously through them. In the end there was not only a clarification of the concept of health but also a concrete proposal for the reform of the German healthcare system. The latter, of course, remained unnoticed. The political mind has created its own rules, and these rules are wedded to self-made compromises (with short periods of expiration), not to a permanent rethinking. At the same time this example again illustrates the way in which science, based on its disciplinary and transdisciplinary competences, is connected to the wider world and what the nature of this connection should be.

Institutional consequences

Theoretical and practical transdisciplinarity, which are increasingly becoming a requirement for theoretical and practical problem solving, while also following the scientific order of the theoretical and the practical, will in future have to lead to new forms of organization in which the boundaries between subjects and disciplines fade into one research perspective. There have long been successful examples, as with the scientific centers in Berkeley, Chicago, Harvard, Princeton, and Stanford, whose work addresses questions that cannot be assigned to a specific subject or discipline, as in the case of the structural research already mentioned.[8] Such centers are also no longer organized according to the traditional structure of physics, chemistry, biology, and other institutes or faculties, but under a transdisciplinary perspective that follows the actual development of science. This is also the case where single problems rather than far-reaching programs are the main focus, as in the case of Bio-X at Stanford[9] or the BIDMC Genomics, Proteomics, Bioinformatics and Systems Biology Center at Harvard.[10] Here biologists use sophisticated physical and chemical methods to elucidate the structure of biologically relevant macromolecules, and physicists such as Nobel laureate Steven Chu, one of the initiators of the Bio-X program, manipulate biological objects with state-of-

8 See L. Garwin, "US Universities Create Bridges between Physics and Biology," *Nature* 397 (January 7, 1999), p. 3.

9 Ibid.

10 See D. Malakoff, "Genomic, Nanotech Centers Open: $200 Million Push by Harvard," *Science* 283 (January 29, 1999), pp. 610–611.

the-art physical methods.[11] Disciplinary competences remain an essential requirement for transdisciplinarily-defined tasks, but they are no longer sufficient to successfully handle research tasks that grow out of the classical subjects and disciplines. And what applies to work on scientific problems should also apply to (scientific) work on the world's problems.

This, however, means that the logic underlying the current institutional development of the scientific system is being questioned. The underlying logic has led to an isolation of subsystems, where networking at a low institutional level should be the slogan, not the expansion of system independences at a high institutional level. This means that temporary institutionalized research groups should replace increasingly isolated scientific subsystems, and that the institutional order of subjects and disciplines must become flexible within a subsystem such as the university. The reasoning is simple from the point of view of research and science: *the system of science must move when research moves.* Currently, things are rather the other way around: research is not seeking its order, but rather an order given by the subsystems and substructures is looking for its research. Such a scientific order, which is wedded to its institutional habits, is counterproductive. This, however, cannot be the future of research and the scientific system. As can be seen, the increasing scientifically-driven transdisciplinarity of scientific research has far-reaching institutional consequences, or should have such consequences.

In particular, this could mean for the university, for example: the dissolution of institute structures, which are usually defined in a narrow manner, in favor of department structures, i.e., those consisting not only in the addition of institute structures, and the strengthening of center structures that follow research requirements. These can also be kept temporarily. Once again, scien-

11 See L. Garwin, "US Universities."

tific structures (organizational structures) must follow research and not vice versa. Collaborative research centers and clusters of a new kind, such as those that are being tested by the German Initiative for Excellence, point in the right direction. We could even imagine a university structure (certainly not as a standard) that is research-oriented and consists solely in centers, with an additional disciplinary-oriented matrix structure for teaching. However, this is but a dream for the future.

Concluding remarks

The game of disciplines with inter- and transdisciplinarity, in analogy to Karl Popper's talk of "the game of science,"[12] is a serious one. Both the scientific (epistemic) and the institutional cards are reshuffled. The times are over in which lecture series between disciplines, or a *studium generale* that supplements the curriculum, fulfilled the need for interdisciplinarity or even transdisciplinarity. Scientists never really took them seriously, that is, with the intention to learn and if necessary to shift the boundaries of subjects and disciplines. But they may still have a certain appeal for a public interested in science. The public only attend them without commitment, to satisfy their academic curiosity and to gain ideas without having to integrate them as part of their own knowledge. And this of course particularly applies if the issue is not only about interdisciplinarity in the usual sense but also transdisciplinarity in the sense described above. This transdisciplinarity could also be described as strong interdisciplinarity, insofar as it is not only an easy, interdisciplinary mingling but a serious cooperation that goes beyond one's own subject and disciplinary boundaries, thereby shifting these boundaries.

12 K. R. Popper, *The Logic of Scientific Discovery*, London etc.: Hutchinson, 1959, p. 53.

It has already been said that the disciplines do not lose their meaning in this process. They form the basis of scientific processes, without which transdisciplinarity in research and teaching would be a vain game with half-truths and alleged metacompetences. In contrast to the common assumption, the concept of a discipline is no less demanding than the concept of transdisciplinarity. We cannot do with a simple distinction between different subject areas, i.e. in epistemic terms, with simple *realistic* assumptions (in the sense of an ontological realism). Nature does not distinguish between physical, chemical, and biological properties in terms of objects specific to each subject or discipline. If physics, chemistry, and biology make the distinction in a disciplinary way, the justification for this must be given on different grounds.

In fact, it is about the constitutive features of the concept of a discipline that are not simply given but are the result of conceptual work. They include norms of object constitution, method explication, and theory building, as well as an interest in knowledge that is methodological and theoretical. When it was previously said that subjects and disciplines are not "natural" but rather something that is historically constrained by the history of science, and whose boundaries are often not theoretical but historical, this does not mean that the significance of subjects, and especially of disciplines, should be underestimated. Rather, this should point to a systematic constitutive task beyond the assumption of realism. Only the fact that this task has been solved in various ways in scientific development, and will probably be solved in a variety of ways in the future, makes the historical character of the building of disciplines.[13] The fundamental role of disciplinary forms of scientific knowl-

13 See C. F. Gethmann, "Disciplinary—Interdisciplinary—Transdisciplinary: A Conceptual Analysis," in C. F. Gethmann et al., *Interdisciplinary Research and Transdisciplinary Validity Claims*, Heidelberg / New York: Springer, 2015, pp. 39–60.

edge remains unaffected, also under transdisciplinary aspects. However, transdisciplinarily-defined tasks at the same time increase the demands on the conceptual clarity of disciplinarity, interdisciplinarity and transdisciplinarity, both in epistemic and institutional terms. This is what the title "From Disciplinarity to Transdisciplinarity and Back Again" was meant to express. The "back" concerns the recovering of a viable disciplinary concept within the context of transdisciplinarity. Science is not easy, even when it is concerned with itself.

Harald Atmanspacher

Transdisciplinary: from a Philosophical Stance to its Implementation

A Response to Jürgen Mittelstrass

Jürgen Mittelstrass belongs to the most influential voices who began to highlight the notion of transdisciplinarity and recommended the viability, power, and necessity of transdisciplinary research as early as 25 years ago.[1] He did so from the perspective of the history and philosophy of science and with respect to science policy and institutional academic structures. In order to understand his specific outlook on transdisciplinarity, it is helpful to understand his philosophical provenance in the Erlangen-Konstanz School, which he formed together with Paul Lorenzen, Kuno Lorenz, Friedrich Kambartel, Peter Janich, and others. These names stand for a scientific constructivism that is complemented by a continuous hermeneutic interpretation of achieved insights and their applications. In his work, Mittelstrass took positions in a number of crucial controversies in modern philosophy of science, such as realism and relativism, the context of discovery and the context of justification, and—notions he coined himself—*homo faber* knowledge (information) and orientation knowledge (wisdom).

1 See J.H. Bernstein, "Transdisciplinarity: A review of its origins, development, and current issues," in *Journal of Research Practice* 11:1 (2015).

In accordance with his constructivist stance, Mittelstrass's position in the realism-relativism debate is inclined toward the relativist side. This means he rejects a fundamentalist realism in which everything the world comprises can be reduced to a fundamental level at which something like fundamental entities (e.g. the particles and fields of physics) are regarded as ultimate building blocks. On the other hand, his arguments along relativist lines of thinking always remain based on a rationality that looks for well-defined relations between descriptive schemes of different disciplines rather than positing them more or less independently, like in a patchwork image. So Mittelstrass is not in contradiction with the idea of a unity of science as long as this is not framed overly reductively.

In this sense his accounts of inter- and transdisciplinarity have a basis in relations between those descriptive schemes utilized by different disciplines. Support for this idea derives from a direction rarely exposed in work on transdisciplinarity: already Willard Van Orman Quine argued that if there is one ontology that fulfills a given description, then there is more than one.[2] In other words, it makes no sense to say what the referents of a description are, beyond saying how to interpret or reinterpret that description in another description.

For Quine, any question as to the "quiddity" (the "whatness") of a thing is meaningless unless a descriptive scheme is specified relative to the thing discussed. The resulting inscrutability of reference is the issue that necessitates regarding any ontology relative to the context of a description—there are no context-free ontologies. The key motif behind this "ontological relativity" is that *any* descriptive level may achieve ontological significance, from elementary particles to ice cubes, bricks,

2 See W.V.O. Quine, "Ontological relativity," in *Ontological Relativity and Other Essays*, New York: Columbia University Press, 1969, pp. 26–68.

tables, and further to thoughts, intentions, volitions, and actions.[3]

This is all fine, relativists may admit, but depending on how closely they lean toward radical versions of constructivism, they may be critical about the notion of an ontology and its assumption of something like a reality out there in the first place. Although Mittelstrass nowhere uses the term reality in his essay, I don't see him aligning with this radical position. It is a challenge to see how we can reasonably talk about a reality of which we know nothing directly, but rather have epistemic access only to patterns that arise in relation to our descriptive tools (including our senses). From Mittelstrass's point of view, this would amount to discussing the constructive basis of the processes through which knowledge is constituted.

Anyway, Quine proposed that a "most appropriate" ontology should be preferred for the interpretation of any particular description, and for this ontology he demands ontological commitment. This leaves us with the challenge of how to determine "most appropriate," and how corresponding descriptive frameworks and their relations to one another are to be identified. Interdisciplinary and in particular transdisciplinary research are options of choice if such relations are to be explicated, reflected, and applied to explore new avenues in scientific research. In this sense, a pluralism of discernibly related descriptive domains with their ontologies is a very appropriate philosophical base for transdisciplinarity.

Before illustrating the innovative power of transdisciplinary approaches in some more detail, I should say that they

3 Quine's proposal was later picked up and developed by Hilary Putnam's "internal" or "pragmatic realism" and by Bas van Fraassen's "constructive empiricism." Notably, both extend the discussion from the purely descriptive into the normative domain; see Hilary Putnam, *The Many Faces of Realism*, LaSalle, IL: Open Court, 1987, and Bas van Fraassen, *The Scientific Image*, Oxford: Clarendon, 1980.

are already helpful if the clarification of established relations between scientific descriptions is at stake. An illustrative example, motivated by Mittelstrass's brief excursion into thermodynamic heat, is the relation between mechanic and thermodynamic descriptions, which featured as a paradigm example of methodological reduction for decades. Meanwhile, a closer and better informed look at the relevant observables from a modern point of view has disproven such reductive claims, and shows that the bridge law connecting mean kinetic energy and temperature is anything other than straightforward.[4] The message of this exercise is that boundaries between disciplines can be better understood through a transdisciplinary study of their mutual relations across the boundary.

Mittelstrass discusses nanotechnology and climate research as two prominent examples of theoretical and practical transdisciplinarity. Let me extend this discussion into the domain of living systems with mental capacities, with theoretical and practical aspects that are of comparable weight. The first is the currently much discussed issue of translational research in biomedical sciences, an example with very practical implications. Such research tries to "translate" results from fundamental molecular biology research into drug development, new medical devices and treatments, preclinical and clinical studies, and ultimately to point-of-care patient applications.

It is obvious that the relevant variables to be investigated at these different stages of research need to be translated *between*

4 For more details see the arguments by Hans Primas, "Emergence in the exact sciences," in *Acta Polytechn. Scandinav.* 91 (1998), pp. 83–98, and the discussion by myself and Peter beim Graben, "Contextual emergence," in *Scholarpedia* 4:3 (2009), p. 7997, accessible at http://www.scholarpedia.org/article/Contextual_emergence. The full subtlety of the bridge law unveils itself as one realizes that its derivation needs thermodynamic equilibrium as a contingent context that must be implemented as a stability condition at the mechanical level. In other words: top-down constraints are needed to complete the bottom-up construction of temperature as a contextually emergent observable from kinetic energy.

the disciplinary domains pertaining to each stage. It is also obvious that the way to do this is not prescribed by any fundamental laws. Together with colleagues from some of the scientific domains involved, we have recently outlined a procedure to systematically identify criteria for relevant variables that is conceptually located *beyond* the involved disciplines.[5] The resulting interplay of "between" and "beyond" expresses the significance of both inter- and transdisciplinary aspects of translational biomedicine in a very evident and concrete fashion.

A key to the relevance question in highly complex biomedical systems is to find descriptive domains of different granularity and construct coarser descriptions in relation to finer ones in a well-defined manner. For instance, many differences between variables at the molecular level (e.g. quantum observables) will be insignificant for variables at the level of organic substances (e.g. classical chirality). As a consequence, the challenge is to identify those fine-grained distinctions that prove meaningful at the coarse-grained level. Similarly, particular variables at the level of animal studies will be insignificant for human-use medication, while others will be significant. If the differences and commonalities in these different domains are properly accounted for, there is a chance to find a successful translational chain from bench to bedside.

My second example is the study of consciousness, a young and striving field in which one of the central capacities of the human (and, likely, more than the human) condition is explored. Its history is interesting, as the term consciousness was completely absent from psychology and cognitive science as long as they were dominated by positivist and behaviorist approaches during the first half of the 20th century. When

5 See Harald Atmanspacher, Ladina Bezzola Lambert, Gerd Folkers, Pius A. Schubiger, "Relevance relations for the concept of reproducibility," in *Journal of the Royal Society Interface* 11 (2014), pp. 2013–2030.

consciousness returned, it reappeared as a scandal—namely with the connotation that it escapes any explanation that could possibly be given by physics, chemistry, biology in general, or brain science in particular. This is testified by phrases such as the "explanatory gap"[6] or the "hard problem of consciousness."[7]

Today, 40 years after Thomas Nagel's paper (as influential as it was philosophically unsophisticated) "What It Is Like to Be a Bat,"[8] the study of consciousness has turned into a highly multi- and interdisciplinary field, most of which has not yet reached the level of transdisciplinarity though. Nevertheless, there are some pertinent novel research directions such as neurophenomenology, with its particular methodological innovations (see Varela 1996, for example).[9] Similarly, subtle versions of dual-aspect monism would be impossible without the integrated efforts of the philosophy of mind, cognitive neuroscience, psychiatry, complex systems theory, and even ideas from quantum theory. Fach et al.[10] indicated some of the ramifications that dual-aspect thinking has for applications concerning mental health and psychiatry.[11]

6 See Frank Jackson, "What Mary didn't know," in *Journal of Philosophy* 83 (1986), pp. 291–295.

7 Cf. David Chalmers, "Facing up to the problem of consciousness," in *Journal of Consciousness Studies* 2:3 (1995), pp. 200–219.

8 See Thomas Nagel, "What Is It Like to Be a Bat," in *The Philosophical Review* 83:4 (1986), pp. 435–450.

9 See Frank Varela, "Neurophenomenology: A methodological remedy for the hard problem," in *Journal of Consciousness Studies* 3:4 (1996), pp. 330–349.

10 See Werner Fach, Harald Atmanspacher, Karin Landolt, Thomas Wyss, Wulf Rössler, "A comparative study of exceptional experiences of clients seeking advice and of subjects in an ordinary population," in *Frontiers in Psychology* 4:65 (2013).

11 Needless to say, Mittelstrass contributed to this discussion as well, and pleaded for a non-Cartesian, and thus non-metaphysical pragmatic dualism as a viable starting point. See Martin Carrier and Jürgen Mittelstrass, *Mind, Brain, Behavior: The Mind-Body Problem and the Philosophy of Psychology*, Berlin: de Gruyter, 1991. One way to develop it would be in terms of dual-aspect thinking.

Remarkably, the study of consciousness would not have taken off so effectively without novel institutional structures: centers rather than traditional departments—a distinction that Mittelstrass puts much emphasis upon. A primary role in this respect was played by the Center for Consciousness Studies at Tucson (Arizona), followed by many other centers with similar scope. Meanwhile the success of their work, the popularity of their topics, and the resounding names of Nobelists affiliated with them have created a clearly recognizable backlash into established academic structures. Transdisciplinary consciousness studies have now become a research focus in numerous standard academic programs in philosophy of mind institutes, psychology and cognitive science departments, brain science faculties, and others.

If this is so, then what makes the organizational structure of a center so special for transdisciplinary research? The way I see it is that centers are not just by themselves more suitable for transdisciplinary research than departments, faculties, institutes, or other established structures. They may be successful simply because they were novel when they were established, and thus provide the opportunity to work with *still* flexible boundaries between *still* connected subunits, and so support the interest-driven dialogue between excellent and inquisitive individuals. But all this may be the hallmark of an initial transient phase that is in danger of decay when structures stabilize and petrify as they develop and grow.

Frankly, I have seen academic centers that were founded with considerable enthusiasm and good will, and scientists with more than proper records, who after ten years faded away into the overadministered and underinspired failure mode of overstrained personnel in positions for which they are unsuitable—as unproductive as one could imagine at any other academic place. I could not agree more with Mittelstrass when he says that "the system of science must move when research moves," but it is no easy task to run an institution in a way that maintains the openness and flexibility of its initial stages.

The lesson I draw from this is that a novel kind of institutional structure alone is no guarantee for successful transdisciplinary research in the long run. I would argue that at least two other factors are decisive as well. First, depending on the size of a research unit, there must be a suitable internal organization with small and interacting subunits, an efficient management that understands itself to be in the service of research (not the other way around), and the persistent willingness to adapt the necessary internal structures and processes to new challenges.

The second factor lies at the human level, a resource hard to overestimate: scientists who are driven by research questions rather than funding, who are keen to understand rather than control, who prefer beneficial advice over rigid instructions, and for whom insight outperforms power. I am aware that these are truisms—but they may be worth emphasizing in an academic world that is more and more governed by economic and political criteria extrinsic to good research and teaching. We need to find ways to counteract this tendency, which somewhat paradoxically can easily take even well-intentioned actions into detrimental effects. If the "chemistry" in a group of such scientists is right, the quality of their work together has the chance to exceed the sum of what each single one of them could possibly achieve.

Florian Dombois

Art with Some T?

A 35-Minute Essay

Contents

1. hic et nunc

This text is written in a book. This book. It was published by the Collegium Helveticum under the joint sponsorship of the University of Zurich (UZH), ETH Zurich, and the Zurich University of the Arts (ZHdK). I am writing for this book. I am not creating a work of art. I am simply writing what I think. What does not appear here in black and white, I did not write. There are no second or third layers of meaning; all that matters is what is here. And that alone. All meaning is contained between these two book covers. Please do not read anything into it.

2. ETHZ–UZH | ZHdK

The present book discusses transdisciplinary research from the perspective of the *trans*—the *beyond*. It is telling that the arts were not mentioned in the invitation to the conference: "To begin with, it is a highly metaphorical concept using a topical notion to locate science," etc. Transdisciplinarity appears to be a scientific opportunity. Not an artistic one. Or is it?

As the Zurich University of the Arts is the Collegium Helveticum's newest sponsor, this certainly requires some thought. Take the following question, for instance: do the arts form a pool of disciplines adjacent to the sciences? Or are they rather found in the *trans*? Are they, in fact, the *beyond*? Or take the following question: do the three institutions—the University of Zurich, ETH Zurich, and the Zurich University of the Arts—form a triangle? Or do ETH Zurich and the University of Zurich form a horizontal axis to which the Zurich University of the Arts is perpendicular, protruding from below? Perhaps you can bear these two lines in mind.

3. Definition of the T

According to Jürgen Mittelstrass, "Transdisciplinarity is research [...] that defines and [...] solves its problems with a view to non-scientific developments, independently of individual disciplines" (original in German).[1] Meanwhile, Klein et al. offer

1 Jürgen Mittelstrass, "Auf dem Wege zur Transdisziplinarität," in *GAIA* 5 (1992), p. 250.

the following definition: "The core idea of transdisciplinarity is different academic disciplines working jointly with practitioners to solve a real-world problem."[2] There may therefore be different approaches from an academic perspective. From the perspective of the arts, I primarily see one commonality: there is a problem to solve.

4. What is a problem?

Everyone has problems nowadays: problems with their work, problems with their lives, and problems with their parents. But this was not always the case. In the past, the problem was a prerogative of academia, signifying a well-defined task of a certain degree of difficulty.[3] Not every difficulty was elevated to the status of a problem. The *problem* was particularly considered to be a *terminus technicus* in three academic fields: geometry, logic, and physics. Here, too, the arts are prominent in their absence—and for good reason. Generally speaking, artists do not solve problems. Forgive me my arrogance, but it is designers who are problem-solvers.

5. Etymology of the problem

The Greek word πρόβλημα, προβλήματος comes from προβάλλειν—literally meaning "throw forward." According to the dictionary,[4]

2 Julie Thompson Klein, Walter Grossenbacher-Mansuy, Rudolf Häberli, Alain Bill, Roland W. Scholz, Myrta E. Welti, *Transdisciplinarity: Joint Problem Solving Among Science, Technology, and Society*, Basel: Birkhäuser, 2001, p. 4.

3 See Helmut Holzhey, "Problem," in *Historisches Wörterbuch der Philosophie*, vol. 7, Basel: Schwabe, 1989, pp. 1397–1408.

4 Wilhelm Gemoll, *Griechisch-deutsches Schul- und Handwörterbuch*, 10th ed., Munich: Oldenbourg Schulbuchverlag, 2006, p. 674.

the word πρόβλημα can be translated in three ways: (1) as a cliff or ledge, (2) militarily: as a shield or defensive weapon, or (3) in the philosophical sense: the academic dispute. Accordingly, we could ask:

If (1) applies, is a problem a cliff from which you must jump?

If (2) applies, is a problem a defensive weapon against unscientific thinking?

If (3) applies, how difficult must a difficulty be before it is defined as a problem? And who determines this? Who decides that a difficulty is sufficiently difficult?

6. Everything flows

In Plato's *Theaetetus* dialogue, Socrates discusses the philosopher Heraclitus and his pupils with Theodorus of Cyrene. Theodorus says: "But if you ask one of them a question, he pulls out puzzling little phrases, like arrows from a quiver, and shoots them off; and if you try to get hold of an explanation of what he has said, you will be struck with another phrase of novel and distorted wording, and you never make any progress whatsoever with any of them, nor do they themselves with one another, for that matter [...]."[5] Does this sound familiar? And does it rather apply to academics or to artists?

7. The other

It has always fascinated me that the Greek philosophers managed without a foreign language. As is well known, a specialist language consisting of foreign words was initially developed

5 Plato, *Theaetetus* 180 a, translated by Harold N. Fowler, *Plato in Twelve Volumes*, vol. 12, Cambridge, MA: Harvard University Press, 1921.

by the Romans, who adopted individual Greek terms and integrated them into Latin. Philosophy without a foreign language: what does it mean for one's thought process when all words are equally familiar? To what do you open yourself if you embed philosophy into everyday language and why do that? Is it autistic or liberating? What does "foreign language" actually mean? And what is *Fremdwort*, a "foreign word," exactly? What a marvelous oxymoron.

8. Verbality

As an artist, I continually find myself struggling for words, such as when I write a text like this one. You will undoubtedly be thinking: "I am no stranger to this problem, myself." But I am not so sure of that. My search for words is not merely hindered by the intricacies of formulating a sentence. It is far more existential in nature. Indeed I also think far outside of language. I have no trouble thinking, but I do not always attach my thoughts to words. Very often I think in sounds, shapes, or spaces. To tell others of these thoughts is therefore already an act of translation, the second step being reflection on the latter. What happens to the meaning of words when their light is scattered through two different media? Can those words still be meaningful?

9. Poetic language

Among the artists, poets and authors strike me as being much like the Greeks. They must create their art with the same terms with which they navigate their daily lives. They express themselves in a medium that is manipulated daily under the dictum of communication, not dissimilar to the Shannon Weaver model: sender—message—receiver. Their sentences are suspected of only saying what their words signify. And perhaps this is indeed true?

10. Pseudo-problems

Analytic philosophy aims to formulate philosophical problems as precisely and unambiguously as possible. This occurs in affirmative statements or so-called "propositions." Once you have expressed a problem as a series of propositions, you can subject these to logical, conceptual or idiomatic analysis. The aim of doing this is either to solve the problem or to expose it as a pseudo-problem. Indeed, that appears to be the main thrust of analytic philosophy: to expose problems as pseudo-problems. I have to ask myself: what is a "pseudo-problem"?

11. Non-propositionality

There is an astonishing term in analytic philosophy: *non-propositionality.* The term signifies everything that cannot be expressed in propositions. The other. The outside. Those who do not belong to us: the outsiders. I am a non-propositionalist, and the concept rather strikes me as a form of philosophical right-wing populism. I cannot believe the word. Is it true? Are those who subscribe to analytic philosophy serious? A word for everything that cannot be conceptualized with their philosophy? I am sorry, but in my opinion "non-propositionality" is a blanket term for everything you do not *want* to conceptualize. Foreigners out. Racist armchair philosophy. Intellectual fascism.

12. The propositional and the poetic

If scientists wish to work with artists, they have no choice but to abandon the safety of the propositional. I would assert that there is no art that can reside in the world of the propositional alone.[6] Indeed, if someone is not prepared to acknowledge the as yet unspoken significance of a statement, they cannot cross over into the *trans* of the arts. I do not mean to say that it would be impossible to compose poetry in a propositional language. On the contrary, excessive sobriety often provides an incredible incentive to read between the lines. Instead I am asserting that an exclusively propositional attitude cannot function as the *beginning* of a cooperation with the arts, but the *end*.

13. Differentiation

Cooperation with the arts requires that you be open to non-propositional thinking. It requires you to abandon the narcissistic rocking chair of certainty in your assertions. You must stand up. You must open the door and leave the house. You must be prepared to think of the space "outside" no longer as "outside" as opposed to "inside," but as the outdoor space that differentiates the landscape on your doorstep. You must be prepared to acknowledge that the sun may also shine in a non-propositional world. You must be able to accept that this other world should not be defined as the negation of what is already known to you. You must be prepared to abandon language.

6 It would be interesting to see whether and how those artists grapple with this problem who still favour an avant-garde line of argument and whose work consists of proving something to be art that was hitherto not considered as such.

14. Barbarism

To the Greeks, a barbarian was someone who spoke unintelligibly—a person who said "bar-bar-bar." The barbarians were all those who did not speak Greek. And these neighboring peoples were assumed to be uneducated, brutish, and wild. The word "barbaric" still carries these connotations today. I am happy to be a bar-bar. It does not surprise me that some consider me to babble—to be someone who eloquently stammers, who contradicts themselves, and who can therefore not speak properly. I am sorry that I am unintelligible. Even I fail to understand much or many, or even myself at times. Yet to condemn the unintelligible is not only arrogant but also symptomatic of a genuine lack of education. It is this arrogance that tripped up the Greeks—herein lay their hubris. For once, the Greeks got it wrong.

15. Multilingual

If we do not wish to simplify to the point of barbarism, we must learn to differentiate other languages that are foreign to us. This is no easy task, however, even among the verbal languages. Are we even capable of organizing our thoughts around different structures to those in our native languages? Do we not always view the languages of others through the prism of our own? What use is a dictionary when we wish to understand a language? What does "understand" even mean? How much time does it take to get to grips with a foreign language? To participate in the language game of the speakers who, as a collective, keep that language alive? Does differentiation not mean giving up the idea of a word-for-word translation in order to jeopardize your own manner of thinking?

16. Many tongues

We must beware of taking the languages metaphor too literally. At best it can be used to assess plausibility: namely that cooperation between scholars and artists constitutes a highly complex situation whose distinction is found not in the respective jargons but in word usage. Perhaps some speak and others do not? Perhaps the differences run far deeper than we currently imagine? In other words, when we see a tongue move, this does not necessarily mean that anything is spoken.

17. Translation

The language in which I wrote this text is German (this here is a translation). It follows a logic of words and sentences structured around a grammar. If I view sound art through this prism, for instance, I can search for comparability. Does the noise correspond to the letter? Does the soundtrack correspond to the word? Does the sound installation correspond to the sentence? Or have I not been taken in by my native language? Are language and sound art even comparable? And if not, what can a translation between incomparable areas achieve?

18. No problems, no language

Perhaps one can think of art as language, but perhaps that is already a form of subordination. At any rate there is the field of art studies, whose work largely consists of "reading" art. Through this interpretative prism, art could be tentatively understood as a language, and perhaps even as a form of knowledge production, as is *en vogue* in "artistic research." From the perspective of reception, I consider the epistemic take on art to be legitimate and not implausible. But I see things rather differently from the perspective of production, as the epistemic assertion is rarely productive. Any artist who attempts to "produce knowledge" with their work must be on their guard. If verbal knowledge pushes ahead of production, the work threatens to devolve into a mere illustration. And that is just one of the problems with this assertion.

19. What is a problem?

Must we always think of research as being fundamentally driven by problems? Indeed, do the sciences not result in many interesting solutions being found before problems are identified for them to solve? And are problems not then designed retrospectively for the solutions? As Theodore Maiman once wrote about his work: "A laser is a solution seeking a problem."[7] And why, in fact, do we always seek solutions? Does this not obligate us to passing time, to progress, and to following the thesis–antithesis–synthesis model? Imagine a world of solutions—a world in which every problem has been solved, in which there are no more questions and no more tasks to complete. Forgive me, but the thought of a world like this fills me with dread. It would be the end. So why is this the world we strive for?

20. Cuckoo!

When you take aim at a problem, you begin a movement that is expected to end with hitting your target. Boom. Stop. Done. Yet when the problem is removed from the equation at the right time, your arrow can continue sailing through the air. As an

7 According to "Theodore Maiman, who built the first laser, dies at 79," in *International Herald Tribune*, May 13, 2007.

artist, I am interested in the second scenario. I can work this way by imagining that my work can continue—that my "solutions" are not exhaustive. I also like to aim for a target when I know that someone will remove the target at the opportune moment. Indeed, experience has shown me that when I really hit something, it is typically not what I had initially aimed for. Perhaps removed targets are pseudo-problems? I would love those.

21. Choreography

If you wish to take seriously the fundamental differences between artistic and academic practice, and if you therefore cannot or do not want to agree on a single, shared problem, you can nonetheless spend a long while working side by side. If I am honest, this is the only kind of transdisciplinarity I believe in—perhaps also because I have worked for some time among both science and humanities scholars. I neither believe in shared problems nor shared solutions. But I enjoy strolling side by side—and not necessarily in my *leisure time*. Here too you can do better or worse. Here too you can trigger a great deal through good casting, good timing, and the right environment; you can freely set something in motion. How and when can which people from which disciplines come together at what places to their mutual benefit? What does it make sense to do to achieve this?

22. *Fahrkunst* (man engine)

In the 19th century, mine shafts were so deep that it took a very long time for workers to enter and exit the mines. In the Harz mountains, the mines plunged to 700 m, meaning it would take at least one hour to descend and two hours to resurface. Wire cable had not yet been invented, so it was not possible to build a lift. Then, the *Berggeschworene* (master miner) Georg Ludwig

Dörell saw the *Kunstknecht* (engineer) Lichtenberg using two reciprocating pump rods to reach a higher level, which inspired him to invent the *Fahrkunst* (man engine) in 1833. The man engine consists of two reciprocating ladders that are driven a few metres up and down by a *Kunstrad* (water wheel) attached to *Kunstgestänge* (flatrods) and a rotating *Kunstkreuz* (cross-shaped lever). When a miner switches sides at the right moment, he can cover considerable distances. Depending on the rhythm of the reciprocating ladders, it is possible to enter and exit the mine shaft with ease.

23. *Fahrkunst:* animation

https://en.wikipedia.org/wiki/Man_engine

If you imagine these ladders as disciplines, they do not have to move far to allow for individual scholars to cover significant distances.

24. The new

Newfoundland was discovered by John Cabot (Giacomo Caboto) in 1497 and was dubbed "newe founde islande"—new for Cabot and new for Europe. The other is always the new. And that is exciting, as it allows you to learn of something beyond your former limits and enter the *trans* space. Let's change perspective a little: let's assume the people who lived in Newfoundland would have considered Cabot and his people to be the new, as for them the Englishmen came from "new-found-land." By labelling someone as "new," you demonstrate that you are ignorant, and this ignorance is very often perfectly symmetrical.

25. Topography

The term "trans" is a relative statement of place meaning "beyond" or "across" from my own here and now. It always depends on where I am speaking from. And perhaps we therefore have to regard this "beyond" not as stable, but as a time-limited concept. In recent years with my working group—composed of an equal number of artists and humanities scholars—I have come to understand the man engine as a change of media and genre. We met and worked together once every four weeks—constantly alternating between a humanities-based approach and an artistic approach. This naturally always put half of the group at a distinct advantage, as they were very familiar with the relevant disciplinary environment. At the next meeting, the advantage was held by the other half of the group. This practice was not merely about getting to know the "other" area and discovering what might be of use in one's own work; it was also about observing how others and oneself operate within their own or an unknown territory.

26. Time

If we define transdisciplinarity not from the perspective of a *terra incognita* but as a process with which to confront your own to the unknown, there are several implications—not least that time becomes a central factor. It is then also no longer simply a question of what, but also of how. It becomes a question of creating conditions under which you can dwell both here and there. And you must also plan in enough time for the change-over and a period of familiarization, time during which you can observe the others and "steal" their ideas. And that is ok, provided that you steal from the other discipline and translate it into your own.

27. Openness to unforeseen results

It is not my job to coax scholars into giving up their problem-based thinking. However, when you view research as "a process driven from behind,"[8] as described by Thomas Kuhn and Hans-Jörg Rheinberger, this begs the question of how anything really new can emerge if you always have a goal in mind? What is so sexy about a well-defined problem?

28. Articulation

As an artist, I do not have to deliver solutions; instead I produce works and make them public. I use the term "articulation" to describe this aspect of my practice. With an exhibition, I articulate from a particular disposition to a specific time and place. It sometimes feels like crystallization in an oversaturated solution. And it is always a matter of what I consider to be the best possible articulation for that given moment; here and now it must be right. Generally speaking, it is not repeatable. But this is why it is always something new—and indeed the more I change myself, the newer it becomes.

29. In the arts

In the past, the fine arts were considered spatial arts and music was considered a temporal art—as in the example of Lessing's 1766 study "Laokoon: An Essay on the Limits of Painting and Poetry." In the 20th century this approach was solidly under-

8 Thomas S. Kuhn, *The Trouble with the Historical Philosophy of Science*, Cambridge, MA: Harvard University Press, 1992, p. 14. Quoted from Hans-Jörg Rheinberger, *Historische Epistemologie. Zur Einführung*, Hamburg: Junius, 2007, p. 90.

mined. The fine arts conquered all possible formats and spaces as they developed performance, happening, video, etc. They became also a temporal art. At the same time music conquered all possible formats and spaces as well; developing new notations and with orchestras arranged in space, it left the concert hall behind and created sound art, etc., thus making it also a spatial art. Both became limitless. Today, we can say that anything can be art and anything can be music. As someone who teaches at the MA Transdisciplinary Studies, MA Fine Arts and MA Composition of Zurich University of the Arts, I ask myself: "Do we even still need *the arts*? Or have we now arrived at the singular concept of *art art*?"

30. Discipline

The term "discipline" is partly responsible for this development. Discipline means punishment. Disciplinary boundaries have been continually challenged and undermined by artists over the last 100 years. And each new attempt to define what art is has, in turn, invited further attempts to undermine this definition. Let us therefore set aside definitional limitations and simply accept that there are no limits. This logically means that there is also no longer any notion of "beyond the limit," and thus the attitude of overcoming limits has begun to lose its appeal. It is boring to claim something supposedly new as art or music. Personally, I am rather more interested in internal limits—the bondage that restricts me within. They do not reduce in number and you cannot simply dispel them or eliminate them altogether; they simply sneak in.

31. When is trans?

Where are the limits and, above all, when are they? What are my personal blind spots, what are the blind spots in my environment and discipline—and where and when do they beleaguer me? And if I turn to face them, where do they escape to next? I believe I have no chance of ever eliminating these blind spots. However, I also feel that not to seek them out, not to want to find them, would drive me mad. Who wants cemented satisfaction? Or a life with a search engine that already knows what kind of answers you want? No, I prefer rather a punishment in the form of a discipline. Rather confrontations with people who think they know what art is, and argument with them. Rather attempt to realize something for yourself and be attacked for it—I know that I am not right, yet to be bogged down in what is wrong would be suffocating.

32. Scientific peer group

There is something that I would gladly steal from academia: the idea of the *peer review*—a concept whereby representatives from a given discipline negotiate among themselves what they deem to be of good quality. Just as in research funding—that of the Swiss National Science Foundation, for instance—other actors in the field are questioned. Doctors are asked what should be researched in medicine. Not medical historians. Not medical critics or patients. The producers of the research, themselves, decide where their search for knowledge should take them next—not the recipients or beneficiaries.

33. Artistic peer group

I know that the peer review process has significant shortcomings—or at least this is what my friends in academia tell me. But look at us in the arts—where the recipients have all the power! For us, art historians at the Swiss National Science Foundation dictate what we should research. For us, art critics and collectors decide which works of art should be valued especially highly, and thus they also influence the awarding of grants, museum acquisitions, and disciplinary prestige. For us, the recipients and beneficiaries of art decide, not the producers. But what would it be like if art was considered from the point of view of the producers? What if we could form some kind of artistic peer group? What if the artist's artist could cut a fine figure? And here I am implicitly advocating a shift in disciplinary terms: one that does not dictate the work or artistic practice, but that is derived from the peer group and its culture of debate. The group of artists who consider themselves musicians could shape music. And the group of artists who consider themselves visual artists could shape the visual arts.

34. Fool

We love the fool for he speaks the truth. And in Tarot his is the first card. He may risk the others, because he risks himself. The fool plays with lives—including his own. Those who discover a gap in reality, from which the ἀ-λήθεια, the unconcealed truth, emerges, is a diabolus—a fallen one. And now the opposite of reproducibility occurs. When you encounter the fool, you must reckon with the unexpected. And this reckoning with the unexpected can, indeed, also mean that you come away empty-handed. And then you find yourself standing there exposed.

35. hic et nunc

This text is written in a book. This book. It was published by the Collegium Helveticum under the joint sponsorship of the University of Zurich, ETH Zurich, and the Zurich University of the Arts. I am writing for this book. I am not creating a work of art. I am simply writing what I think. What does not appear here in black and white, I did not write. There are no second or third layers of meaning; all that matters is what is here. And that alone. Even if it hurts me. All meaning is contained between these two book covers. Please do not read anything into it.[9]

9 This paper was translated by Paul Skandera.

Amrei Wittwer

Artists and the Transdisciplinary Workplace

A Commentary

Florian Dombois is questioning the role of artists, here and today at this institute. Are they excluded from scientific inter- or transdisciplinary practice? I am grateful for Florian Dombois's rich, inspiring lecture, and I thank him for a definition of transdisciplinarity by Julie Klein:

> Different academic disciplines working jointly with practitioners to solve a real-world problem.

This definition describes the actual field of research on ADHD in children, a field of research I have been trying to contribute to for the last four years. Problems in this field are real-world problems that have to be solved by the cooperation of different disciplines, together with practitioners, and especially with the party concerned, the children. Solutions and knowledge in this field can contribute to support children, a group most worthy of protecting.

Unfortunately, artists cannot find a home in this field of research as described by Florian Dombois. The reason lies in three of his propositions, given here in my own words, two of which cannot be fulfilled by a transdisciplinary study on ADHD in children.

- Artists do not solve problems.
- Artists don't need a common language.
- Artists need the grey zone.

Artists solve no problems

Cocaine, one of the most addictive of the illegal drugs, with the strongest reinforcement, has a pharmacological mechanism that is almost identical to methylphenidate (Ritalin), one of the most commonly prescribed psychiatric drugs for children.[1] The practice of treating children with ADHD with dangerous drugs could only be justified if ADHD was an idiopathic, medical problem. However, ADHD is no physical disease but *unwanted behavior*[2] that can be understood as *educational underperformance*.

Parents want their children to be successful. Parents and teachers believe that children need the diagnosis and drugs. Therefore stimulating drugs are given to healthy children in order to produce a more obedient or sociable character and to start the (evidently futile) attempt to improve the academic performance of the children. Is this not problematic?

Evidence shows that:

1) Children are diagnosed with ADHD although they have no illness or disease.[3]
2) Diagnosis itself is harming the children.[4]

1 *Archives of General Psychiatry* 52.6 (1995), p. 422.

2 S. Timimi, "ADHD is best understood as a cultural construct," in *Br J Psychiatry* 184 (2004), pp. 8–9, http://dx.doi.org/10.1192/bjp.184.1.8; Iain McClure, "ADHD is a Behavioural Construct, Not a Psychiatric Condition," in *BMJ* 347 (2013), p. 7071f.

3 E. R. Coon, R. A. Quinonez, V. A. Moyer, and A. R. Schroeder, "Overdiagnosis: How Our Compulsion for Diagnosis May Be Harming Children," in *Pediatrics* 134(5) (2014), p. 1015; Iain McClure, "ADHD is a Behavioural Construct."

4 S. P. Hinshaw, *The Mark of Shame: Stigma of Mental Illness and an Agenda for Change*, New York: Oxford University Press, 2007.

3) Children do not systematically participate in the diagnosis, and are not systematically informed.[5] There is strong evidence that this may be illegal,[6] and can lead to claims for physical and psychological damages.[7]
4) Therapy with stimulant drugs normally has no therapeutic effect,[8] and is harming the children.[9] Ignoring this empirical evidence may lead to the physician's responsibility for bodily harm.[10]

Artists need no common language

How can a complex problem be solved?

Without the focus on a common scientific paper or other products, no transdisciplinary cooperation is possible. (Hans Rudolf Heinimann) It is obvious that in order to solve complex problems like ADHD, which involve different disciplines like

5 American Psychiatric Association, *Diagnostic and Statistical Manual of Mental Disorders*, DSM, 5th ed., Washington: American Psychiatric Publ., 2013; "Verhaltens- und emotionale Störungen mit Beginn in der Kindheit und Jugend (F90-F98)," Deutsches Institut für Medizinische Dokumentation und Information, World Health Organization, *The ICD-10 Classification of Mental and Behavioural Disorders*, Geneva: WHO.

6 Convention on children's rights, see A. Kratschmar, "Die Rechte von Kindern und Jugendlichen," http://www.kinderrechte.gv.at/wp-content/uploads/2015/08/Broschuere-Kinderrechte_Web_DS_mit-neuer-Karte.pdf (accessed May 2, 2017).

7 BGH NJW 2007, p. 2771f. The legal situation in Austria and Switzerland is similar to that of Germany.

8 O.J. Storebø, H. B. Krogh, E. Ramstad et al., "Methylphenidate for attention-deficit/hyperactivity disorder in children and adolescents: Cochrane systematic review with meta-analyses and trial sequential analyses of randomized clinical trials," in *BMJ* 351 (2015); B. Molina, "The MTA at 8 Years: Prospective Follow-Up of Children Treated," in *J Am Acad Child Adolesc Psychiatry* 48(5) (May 2009), pp. 484–500.

9 "Safety of Psychotropic Drugs in Children and Adolescents," in *Pharmacovigilance in Psychiatry*, Springer International Publishing, 2016, pp. 257–283.

10 §§ 223ff. StGB.

medicine, pedagogy, pharmacy, psychology, sociology, ethics, or law, a *common language* is the *conditio sine qua non*. Of course a *common goal* is also necessary. In a research project on ADHD the common goal has to be the wellbeing of the affected children.

Cooperation is easily flawed, however, if a goal is incongruent with commercial interests. Unfortunately, evidence shows that the social view of ADHD, its diagnoses and therapy are biased mostly by commercial and not by public interests.[11] Conflicts of interest are suspected to be the drivers of bad diagnostic and therapeutic practice as well as poor research: physicians,[12] researchers,[13] and also some teachers[14] have been heavily criticized when it comes to ADHD. Disease-mongering seems to be an important driver for a derelict, body-centered model of disease, and of the myth of the existence of universal bodily markers for ADHD.

One step in the right direction is to accept that *ADHD is not a medical but a pedagogical problem* that needs pedagogical, educational solutions. It is necessary to accept that in the case of ADHD the area of conflict is usually not the body of the child but the *conflicted relationship with adults*.[15] Important measures are:

11 R. Moynihan, D. Henry, "The Fight against Disease Mongering: Generating Knowledge for Action," in *PLoS Med* 3(4) (2006), p. 3.
12 https://correctiv.org/recherchen/euros-fuer-aerzte/
13 John Ioannidis, "The Mass Production of Redundant, Misleading, and Conflicted Systematic Reviews and Meta-Analyses," in *The Milbank Quarterly* 94.3 (2016), pp. 485–514.
14 C. B. Phillips, "Medicine Goes to School: Teachers as Sickness Brokers for ADHD," in *PLoS Med* 3(4) (2006), p. 182.
15 P. Breggin, *The Ritalin Fact Book*, Cambridge, MA: Perseus Publishing, 2002.

- The pedagogical and psychological training of parents and teachers,[16,17] e.g. behavioral and psychosocial training.[18,19,20]
- Educational measures and coachings for children that identify their gaps of knowledge and foster their enthusiasm for learning.[21]
- Psychoeducation of parents and teachers, e.g. on nutrition,[22] sports, and the regulation of media consumption.[23]

Artists need grey zones

There is no abundance of grey zones in the research on ADHD. All science is a rude simplification. We can only try to improve

16 Russell A. Barkley et al., "The efficacy of problem-solving communication training alone, behavior management training alone, and their combination for parent–adolescent conflict in teenagers with ADHD and ODD," in *Journal of Consulting and Clinical Psychology* 69.6 (2001), p. 926.

17 Hannes Brandau and Wolfgang Kaschnitz, *ADHS im Jugendalter: Grundlagen, Interventionen und Perspektiven für Pädagogik, Therapie und Soziale Arbeit*, Weinheim: Beltz Juventa, 2013.

18 Morris Zwi et al., "Parent training interventions for Attention Deficit Hyperactivity Disorder (ADHD) in children aged 5 to 18 years," in *Cochrane Library*, 2011.

19 Russell A. Barkley et al., "A comparison of three family therapy programs for treating family conflicts in adolescents with attention-deficit hyperactivity disorder," in *Journal of Consulting and Clinical Psychology* 60.3 (1992), p. 450.

20 J. Frölich, M. Döpfner, H. Biegert and G. Lehmkuhl, "Praxis des pädagogischen Umgangs von Lehrer/innen mit hyperkinetisch-aufmerksamkeitsgestörten Kindern im Schulunterricht," in *Praxis der Kinderpsychologie und Kinderpsychiatrie*, 2013, p. 501.

21 P. Breggin, *The Ritalin Fact Book*.

22 Edmund J.S. Sonuga-Barke et al., "Nonpharmacological interventions for ADHD: systematic review and meta-analyses of randomized controlled trials of dietary and psychological treatments," in *American Journal of Psychiatry* 170 (3) (2013).

23 Sanne W. C. Nikkelen et al., "Media use and ADHD-related behaviors in children and adolescents: A meta-analysis," in *Developmental Psychology* 50.9 (2014), p. 2228.

the complex reality of about 42,000 (5% of 800,000) afflicted Swiss children and teens. Cooperation with artists could contribute to an emotional and cognitive transfer of knowledge.

Conclusion

Finally one of the first utilizations of the word "Kunst" in Grimm's *Deutsches Wörterbuch*:

> Er blickt sie an durch kunstes glas,
> er wist (erkannte) wie sie genaturet was.[24]

> He watches her though artificial glass,
> He recognizes what her nature was.

Florian Dombois, how can artists be involved in productive, transdisciplinary cooperation? What has to be avoided, what is conducive?

24 *Ambraser Liederbuch*, 1582.

Andrea B. Braidt

Transgressing Disciplines

The Transdisciplinary Settings of Media Studies, Gender Studies, and Artistic Research

Transdisciplinary has lost its scientific glamour. Gone are the days when philosophers and mathematicians developed research in unison; when the transgression of disciplinary borders implied academic provocation (at the traditional institutions of research) or even treason. Transdisciplinary thinking has become a mainstream request by the ministries of sciences. Scholars of all disciplines are requested to work on the "Big Challenges" of the Horizon 2020 program, and are required to do so in transdisciplinary (and trans-European) research settings.[1] To develop research questions within a single discipline is, so it seems, reminiscent of the last century. Or even the century before. But what implications does the inevitable transdisciplinary working program have for the development of specific disciplines? How are new—or relatively new—disciplines shaped by a scientific climate that demands the transgression of disciplinary limits?

In the following I will look at the settings in which the transdisciplinary thinking works as a *constituent* aspect of a number

1 The EU research framework program Horizon 2020, running from 2014 until 2020, is "challenge-based" and focuses its funding on seven societal challenges: health/demographic change, food security/sustainability, efficient energy, green transport, climate action, reflective societies, and secure societies. See https://ec.europa.eu/programmes/horizon2020/en/h2020-section/societal-challenges (accessed March 3, 2017).

of disciplines. I will look at media studies and gender studies as examples of research areas that were "founded" as transdisciplinary disciplines—and that to a certain degree have remained transdisciplinary "by nature." Both disciplines have rapidly developed over the last three decades—maybe as a result of their transdisciplinarity?

Artistic research, and this is the third disciplinary setting that interests me, has developed in a similar way. Artistic research, which consists of generating knowledge and insight by applying artistic methods to explicit research questions, is often seen as a prototypical transdisciplinary field of experimentation, an area where the sciences and art combine into one, and where scientists (i.e. natural scientists) seem to consider themselves as universal aesthetic geniuses, much like Leonardo da Vinci. But this way of looking at artistic research is, I argue, not informed by contemporary artistic production and discourse, but rather by the desire to aestheticize hard science. I want to look at artistic research—following the example of gender and media studies—as a transdisciplinary field that has developed as an autonomous artistic discipline.

When I was writing my book on the transgression of gender and genre in narrative film about nine years ago—developing an idea that I would come to call "trans-genus"[2]—I did so from the perspective of feminist film theory, that is, the nexus of gender studies and media studies. I looked at how the narrative constructions of gender and genre are interlinked. I formulated the hypothesis that in transgressive moments of gender, genre is also prone to moments of transgression. The reason for this simultaneous transgression is, I found, quite obvious: film narrative, like any narrative, is as much gendered as it is generic—expressed in generic terms. So if the film narrative

2 Andrea B. Braidt, *Film-Genus: Gender und Genre in der Filmwahrnehmung*, Marburg: Schüren, 2008.

itself is brought to its limits, then gender and genre constructions also transgress.

Transgressive narrative moments in film occur when the music takes over and subordinates all other signifying elements. These moments, which I call "musical numbers," can be found not only in musicals but in many narrative films, and are sometimes referred to as "American montage"—a sequence of shots indicating a long elapse of time and some sort of narrative development, usually of the protagonist, as seen, for example, in the montage sequences in the ROCKY films (six sequels to the initial 1976 film, the latest from 2015), which show Rocky Balboa in his training routine, accompanied by the famous theme song. Sometimes musical numbers are realized in the credit or title sequence, such as those found in James Bond movies or in the famous opening scene of JACKIE BROWN (USA, 1997), where Jackie, a flight attendant (played by Pam Grier), rolls along the moving sidewalk at the airport while the song "Across 110th Street" plays. Occasionally, actual musical numbers are realized within the diegetic world of the narrative (e.g. karaoke scenes), or sometimes as scenes where the protagonists suddenly break out into song and dance even though the film has not been identified as a musical film, as in François Ozon's 8 FEMMES (France, 2002), for example. And sometimes the musical scenes play out as moments when pop hits kick in and take over in such a fundamental way as to turn everything else into a non-narrative imaging, like Simon and Garfunkel's song "The Sound of Silence," which plays in Mike Nichols's THE GRADUATE (USA, 1967) after Benjamin Braddock (played by Dustin Hoffmann) has sex for the first time with Mrs. Robinson (played by Anne Bancroft).

These instances in film have the potential to negotiate gender and genre norms and conventions. Focusing on the norms and conventions of gender and genre in films makes their boundaries visible, and questions the basis of their very existence. Transgression of the border, as described in Michel

Foucault's famous text "A Preface to Transgression" (1974) does remove the border but indicates its constructedness. He said: "Transgression forces the limit to face the fact of its imminent disappearance, to find itself in what it excludes (perhaps, to be more exact, to recognize itself for the first time), to experience its positive truth in its downward fall."[3]

To talk about these transgressions in my book, I looked not only at Foucault's text but also at Mikhail Bakhtin's notion of the carnivalesque as a transgressive, topsy-turvy time and space. I used Barbara Johnson's gender/genre text and many other philosophical and/or philological theories to talk about the phenomenon of transgression in narrative film. Gender theories from feminist traditions informed my thinking about the constructedness of gender, from psychoanalytic models following (and critiquing) Laura Mulvey's concept of spectatorship to Linda Williams's body genres, and, of course, Judith Butler's performativity thesis. Looking closer at the films themselves, I turned to film narratology and film-genre theories—from Emilie Altenloh to the Russian formalists to ideas put forward by Rick Altman and Steve Neale, and, of course, to the neo-formalist school of David Bordwell and Kristin Thompson. The empirical method I proposed in my work to falsify and verify my hypothesis was a method derived from psychology: the "Heidelberger Strukturlegetechnik," developed by Brigitte Scheele and Norbert Groeben.[4] This method would permit me to operationalize the textual hypotheses that were formulated on the basis of the-

3 Michel Foucault, "A Preface to Transgression," in Michel Foucault, *Language, Counter-Memory, Practice: Selected Essays and Interviews*, ed., trans. Donald F. Bouchard, Ithaca: Cornell University Press, 1977, p. 34. The original French text appeared in 1963 in the journal *Critique* (special edition on Georges Bataille), reprinted in *Préface à la transgression*, Paris: Éditions Lignes, 2012.

4 Brigitte Scheele and Norbert Groeben, *Die Heidelberger Struktur-Lege-Technik (Slt): Eine Dialog-Konsens-Methode zur Erhebung subjektiver Theorien mittlerer Reichweite* [Beiheft Zum Legekasten], Weinheim, Basel: Beltz Verlag, 1984.

oretical thinking into a structured interaction with recipients in order to gain insight into the function of gender and genre when looking at films. Qualitative interviews allow the "subjective theories" that recipients use when looking at media texts to be brought forward, and the method even provides a tool kit to visualize these subjective theories through structural images.[5]

With this brief sketch of a research project undertaken in media studies, I want to provide an example of the transdisciplinary nature of the discipline. Like many disciplines in the humanities and social sciences, media studies does not have a given set of theories and methods that scholars use when formulating their research questions. The variety of methods used to research film, for example, range from traditional psychoanalytic models, following Sigmund Freud and Jacques Lacan or Carl Jung, to the neo-formalism of David Bordwell, Wolfgang Beilenhoff, and others; methods are derived from social sciences—Pierre Bourdieu's ideas and of course Bruno Latour's actor-network theory—or from literary theory that looks at the film as text (e.g. Helmut Korte, Klaus Kanzog, and many others). Poststructuralist philosophy should also be mentioned, especially the writings of Gilles Deleuze or the technical history of media following Friedrich Kittler. The methods used within media studies have become so widespread that attending the annual conference of media studies, organized by the GfM Gesellschaft für Medienwissenschaft, which brings together German-speaking media scholars, has become a Babylon-like experience in which only limited numbers of scholar-groups speak the same language of theoretical paradigms. And what is true for the range of methods is even more true for the contexts in which theories about research problems are formulated. Contemporary media studies raises the question about the object of study itself, the question of what constitutes media.

5 See my *Film-Genus.*

Proponents of media studies may refute the idea of calling it a "discipline" altogether, and Claus Pias asks what it is in the title of his 2010 book *Was waren Medien?*[6] This undisciplined sense of a discipline has been celebrated in media studies, certainly ever since Paul Feyerabend wrote his 1976 text "Wider den Methodenzwang," and in many ways rightly so. Media— just like the world— are something "generally unknown" (in Feyerabend's words).[7] New media are continually coming into existence, even as we speak: new TV formats are screened all the time, new web-based media devices, apps, social media platforms, and so on develop much faster than a discipline can research them. So being restricted to a closed set of methods and theories would mean that scholars of a disciplined discipline could only deal with what already exists, and this is not an option for media studies. So media studies is extremely undisciplined and is thus extremely transdisciplinary, transgressing its boundaries with almost every move.

Maybe this is why media studies is currently one of the most popular disciplines with students in BA, MA, and doctoral programs in Germany and Austria (there are four thousand students enrolled in theater, film and media studies at the University of Vienna, for example). This is quite astonishing for a discipline that seems to be almost impossible to define, a discipline in which institutional disciplinary gatekeepers, such as introductory publications supposed to give an insight into what the discipline actually is, call the sense of discipline into question themselves, like "Was mit Medien?" in the legendary red-blue UTB canonical series, quoting the wish of many university aspirants to study something "with media."

6 Claus Pias, ed., *Was waren Medien?*, Zurich: diaphanes, 2010.
7 Paul Feyerabend, *Wider den Methodenzwang*, Frankfurt am Main: Suhrkamp, 1976, p. 17.

Media studies is also, I claim, "naturally" transdisciplinary because it was founded as a disciplinary transgression by scholars in traditional fields like philology, language studies, social sciences, philosophy, or history turning to film—and later to the media—out of scholarly curiosity and certainly also necessity. Before media studies departments were founded as discrete entities, film and media studies were usually projects by scholars from different departments coming together to teach courses on film or to build additional curricula on media studies. In the 1980s in the United Kingdom and the United States, and during the late 1990s in Europe, departments were formed and study programs created. But of course the scholars who were historians, philosophers, or philologists carried the "avant-garde" sense of the transdisciplinary transgression with them. It is only during the last ten years that media studies "natives" have increasingly been given teaching positions in media studies, indicating the acceptance of the discipline in academic circles and institutions.

At roughly the same time as media studies developed as a transdisciplinary discipline, gender studies emerged (then usually called "women's studies") during the 1970s at the nexus of political, social, cultural sciences, and the humanities. Like media studies, gender studies did not claim a limited set of methods and theories, and similarly has had a pretty successful career. But unlike media studies, gender studies is rooted in a political movement.

It would take too much time and space to fully describe the process of how gender studies evolved out of the second wave of the women's movement in the late 1960s—the first, of course, being the suffragette movement at the beginning of the twentieth century—and the critique of the systematic exclusion of women from political, social, economic, and scientific projects. This critique, formulated by literary scholars, sociologists, political scientists, and historians, carried with it a by-product that questioned itself more and more: the insistence on the inclusion of women perpetuated the idea of a binary order of gender structured by a hierarchy of power that was more important than other hierarchical differences, like race, class, or sexuality. Women's studies and the women's movement of the 1970s produced a form of identity politics that could only include the analysis of difference by adding on the categories of struggle. Paradigmatically, the turn from women's studies to gender studies was proposed in "Gender: A Useful Category for Historical Analysis" (1986), written by the American historian Joan W. Scott. Scott calls for a definition of gender as a "constitutive element of social relationships based on perceived differences between the sexes" and as "a primary way of signifying relationships of power."[8] She elaborates this definition of gender by an interrelation of four elements:

1) cultural signifiers that evoke binary (and often contradictory) gender representations (e.g. Mary and Eve);
2) normative concepts that provide ways of interpreting the symbols;
3) politics and social institutions that bring forth the binaries of gender relations;
4) the perspective on gender as a subjective identity.[9]

Scott lays the ground for what would be called "constructivist feminist theorizing," which would become a theory highlighted in the 1990s through writings such as Butler's scholarly bestsellers *Gender Trouble: Feminism and the Subversion of Identity* (1990) and *Bodies That Matter: On the Discursive Limits of "Sex"* (1993).[10] Today it seems hardly possible that a scholarly

8 Joan W. Scott, "Gender: A Useful Category for Historical Analysis," in *American Historical Review* 91, no. 5 (December 1986), p. 1067.
9 Ibid., pp. 1067–1068.
10 See Judith Butler, *Gender Trouble: Feminism and the Subversion of Identity*, New York: Routledge, 1990; and *Bodies That Matter: On the Discur-*

project in gender studies, from whatever disciplinary perspective undertaken—be it medicine or philosophy, history or social sciences, law or philology, history of science, biology, or quantum physics—could be undertaken without a mention of Butler's thesis on the performativity of gender identity. This thesis constitutes a disciplinary core of gender studies, a scientific paradigm in the sense that was described by Thomas Kuhn as a kind of "object for further articulation and specification under new or stricter conditions."[11] In a similar vein, Astrid Deuber-Mankowsky has claimed that gender as an analytic category could and should be conceptualized as an "epistemic thing," following Hans-Jörg Rheinberger's claim that[12] the category is "more than an object but structures, reactions, functions which are open, question generating, and complex."[13]

So what is transdisciplinary about gender studies? Well, apart from the epistemic thing called gender, any description of gender studies is confronted with a multitude of research questions, methodologies, theoretical contextualization of the paradigmatic notion of performative gender identity, and disciplinary points of departures. And a certain set of rifts or divides that are well kept—and well loved—by the scientific gender studies community. One of these is certainly the divide between the philosophical fraction and the social science fraction of gender studies, with their respective disciplinary relatives.

sive Limits of "Sex," New York: Routledge, 1993.

11 Thomas S. Kuhn, *Die Struktur wissenschaftlicher Revolutionen*, 2nd ed., trans. Hermann Vetter, Frankfurt am Main: Suhrkamp, 1976, p. 37.

12 Hans-Jörg Rheinberger, *Experimentalsysteme und epistemische Dinge: Eine Geschichte der Proteinsynthese im Reagenzglas*, Frankfurt am Main: Suhrkamp, 2006.

13 Rheinberger, cited in Astrid Deuber-Mankowsky, "Gender – Ein epistemisches Ding? Zur Geschichtlichkeit des Verhältnisses von Natur, Kultur, Technik und Geschlecht," in *Was kommt nach der Genderforschung? Zur Zukunft der feministischen Theoriebildung*, ed. Rita Casale and Barbara Rendtorff, Bielefeld: transcript, 2008, p. 170.

Another is the divide—and this is due to the historical roots of gender studies and the acrimonious fights about the political implications of feminist theorizing—between the "practitioners" and the "theorists" of gender studies. Practitioners are professionals dealing with processes of gender mainstreaming in institutions—also of course in research institutions—who are building upon gender research and trying to operationalize gender theory into measures that can be undertaken for the advancement of women and the abolition of discrimination against those who suffer from the binary gender system. And maybe this setting between basic research and applied research, known to almost every scientific discipline, is particularly transgressive in the field of gender studies.

In many ways, media studies and gender studies are, it seems to me, characterized by disciplinary transgressiveness. Whereas media studies has been established from many different disciplines, and as a consequence has developed a disciplinary identity as a multifaceted, transdisciplinary project—which by no means claims to have a common object of study, not even the study of the term that forms the first part of its name—gender studies has brought forth a scientific paradigm that most proponents of the discipline would agree upon to be the point of departure for their scientific work. Still, gender studies is transdisciplinary because of the fact it has been mainstreamed in all scientific disciplines and has become an organizational requirement for many political, social, and scholarly institutions in terms of plans to decrease discrimination effected by gender difference.

Artistic research, my third example of a transgressive discipline, shows yet another setting of transdisciplinarity. Let me start by using Anna Artaker's project COUNTERPARTS as an example:

> COUNTERPARTS takes Benjamin's mimetic thinking as a working principle: it brings together images of man-made constructions

that are linked by similar forms, but separated by their affiliation to different contexts and historical epochs. By crossing the images, COUNTERPARTS directly renders Benjamin's philosophical concept productive on a sensual that is visual level. In this sense it is a perfect example of artistic research: the method for revealing new aspects and sparking new insights about the constructions we see is an artistic one, involving a precise selection of images as well as a form of montage—the interchange of puzzle pieces—that remains true to the provisional character of Benjamin's writings and translates them into art.[14]

Artistic research arguably takes its point of departure from the artistic practices of conceptualism, which reaches back to Marcel Duchamp and gains wide recognition with the work of Lawrence Weiner, Ed Ruscha, Sol LeWitt, and many others. In the 1960s the artwork as a commodified and commodifiable object underwent a fundamental critique, whereby artistic expression was materialized in the description of a process or in the development of an idea that brought the artistic intervention forward. This focus on the process of how art produces insight and critical knowledge about aesthetic, social, political, and, of course, institutional conditions and conditionings prompts the notion of doing research through artistic means. Artistic practices, with their unsurpassable ability to condense a thought or idea, started to be seen as tools for systematic inves-

14 Anna Artaker in an e-mail to the author. More information on the COUNTERPARTS project can be found on the artist's website: http://anna-artaker.net/pdf/MappeENG_2003–15_WEB.pdf (accessed March 6, 2017). See also Anna Artaker, Meike Schmidt-Gleim, "The New in the Guise of the Old, the Old in the Guise of the New. Two examples from the COUNTERPARTS Series" and Martí Peran, "COUNTERPARTS," both in Martí Peran (ed.), *Futurs abandonats. Demà ja era la qüestió* [Abandoned Futures. Tomorrow Was Already the Question], exh. cat. Fabra i Coats Centre d'art contemporani de Barcelona, 2014, pp. 10–13.

tigation, rather than as aesthetic and purely self-referential (thus disciplinary) expressions.

Mary Kelly's *Post-Partum Document* (1973–79), for example, explores and researches the relationship between mother and child by showing objects that are signifiers of the construction of this relationship (e.g. stained diapers, children's garments, etc.) as aesthetic objects. The artifacts are not only representations of the results of research but also use the artistic context, the conventional setting of the gallery and the perception mode (aesthesis) as tools for an engagement with society at large.

> What is constructed by the installation is not a technical, scientifically tested and publicly disseminated result, but rather the production of a relationality between subject and object which questions the process of construction itself. [...] By turning the "child" into the object of scientific exploration in a quite literal way, Kelly exposes the reproductive work [of the mother] as part of the social production and reveals the ostensibly rational and epistemologically driven research as a logic of utilization by connecting it to processes of subjectification and social inclusions and exclusion.[15]

Projects like Kelly's led to a development of artistic research as an endeavor that explicitly relates to how research processes in other disciplines are shaped: a research question is formulated that is explicitly situated in the "state-of-the-art" respective field of artistic inquiry; an artistic method for undertaking the research is chosen; interim results are presented to a fellow community of professionals in the field (of art and artistic research); the final results are disseminated through appropri-

15 Anette Baldauf and Ana Hoffner, "Kunst-basierte Forschung und methodischer Störsinn," in *Critical Studies: Kultur- und Sozialtheorie im Kunstfeld*, ed. Elke Gaugele and Jens Kastner, Vienna: Springer, 2015, p. 330ff.

ate channels[16]—which, of course, usually look different from printed peer-reviewed journals, as they need to allow for many forms of expression. But arts-based research, defined by Anette Baldauf and Ana Hoffner in the quote above, has a decidedly irreverent take on these processes of scientific "normalization": "Art-based research projects pick at modern understandings of science and its master narratives; they challenge the Western, modern research ethos making use of unconventional methods. Their promise is that of unsettlement: critical art-based research wants to tear holes into the matrix of understanding, establish irritating connections and dissolve conventions of saturation."[17]

Although Baldauf and Hoffner take the emphasis on an unsettlement maybe a little too far, and claim that the stakes are too high, many scholars argue for the epistemological potential of artistic research in a similar vein. In his text "What Is at Stake? Qu'est-ce que l'enjeu? Paradoxes, Problematics, Perspectives in Artistic Research Today,"[18] ZHdK's Giaco Schiesser draws upon Gaston Bachelard's non-Cartesian epistemology and Rheinberger's process epistemology to come up with what he thinks is the building block of artistic research's epistemology: "It has become very obvious that artistic research is a *singular explor-*

16 For example, the online research catalogue developed by the Society of Artistic Research, see https://www.researchcatalogue.net/ (accessed November 19, 2016).

17 Baldauf and Hoffner, "Kunst-basierte Forschung und methodischer Störsinn," p. 327 (translation by Baldauf). Original German: "Kunstbasierte Forschungen [...] kratzen am modernen Wissenschaftsverständnis und ihren Meistererzählungen; sie fordern den westlichen, modernen Forschungsethos mittles unkonventionellen Methoden heraus. Ihr Verheissen ist das einer Verstörung: kritische künstlerische Forschungen wollen Löcher in die Matrix des Verstehens reissen, irritierende Verbindung herstellen und konventionelle Nahtstellen trennen."

18 Giaco Schiesser, "What Is at Stake? Qu'est-Ce Que L'enjeu? Paradoxes, Problematics, Perspectives in Artistic Research Today," in *Art, Research, Innovation and Society*, ed. Gerald Bast and Elias G. Carayannis, Vienna: Springer, 2015, p. 202 (emphasis in original).

ative research, a discovery of and dealing with 'gaps,' the 'precarious,' the 'unstable,' or the 'inadequate,' etc., in each single case, instead of building *hypotheses* that are made verified/falsified (like in the sciences) or *theses* that have to be argued and made plausible (like in the humanities). And that these singular explorations are based on what [...] I would call 'intuition' perceived as 'condensed experienceness' (*verdichtete Erfahrenheit*)."

This definition, resting partly on Dieter Mersch's notion of the "singular experience," is in my view particularly important for its implied inclusiveness. The singular explorations based on condensed experienceness could be seen as the artistic competence, formed by and through the respective disciplinary artistic practice, of the researcher. In the case of my initial example, Artaker's *Counterparts*, the visual competence of the visual artist is her ability to perceive the visual state of the world in a condensed form. In her project, she undertakes a singular exploration of structural visual kinships using the technique of photographic montage as a research method. Artaker and Meike Schmidt-Gleim's research is also transdisciplinary, in that they use Walter Benjamin's conceptualization of mimetic thinking as a trigger for their artistic process. And it is also perhaps an argument against Schiesser, because COUNTERPARTS develops the idea that everything is interconnected, that all human and natural activities somehow bear a resemblance.

So what is transdisciplinary about artistic research? Many would argue that to talk about disciplines in art has long been surpassed by artistic practices that are developed through impulses (or questions) that come from outside of art and are thus not shaped by a disciplinary setting. Many art universities have, as a consequence, stopped organizing their departments and study programs in disciplines like painting, sculpture, film, photography, and so on, but via other means, like dimensions (1D, 2D, 3D, 4D) or topics, giving the students the opportunity to explore their full potential and range of artistic expression.

But rather than being transdisciplinary, this tendency often proposes a nondisciplinary perspective of developing artistic practices and, as a consequence, artistic research.

At the Academy of Fine Arts Vienna, we still hold on to a studio system built on disciplinary organization (contextual painting, abstract painting, figurative painting, contextual sculpture, performative sculpture, video installation, digital media, and so forth), which is accompanied by a structure of analogue and digital workshops ranging from wood to computer to plaster, metal, textile, digital, and many more, also including a drawing class (*Abendakt*). Students are free to stay in one studio for their entire studies or change studios every semester; the enormous international interest in the academy to a large extent rests on this (non-Bolognarized) organizational structure. Artistic research—in terms of study programs, only carried out at the doctoral level—builds upon this disciplinary undergraduate education and enables a transdisciplinary development of research projects.

What the discourse about transgressing disciplinary borders needs is differentiation. As I have shown in describing three transdisciplinary settings, the conditions and practices that media studies, gender studies, and artistic research are confronted with vary greatly in terms of posing research questions, formulating basic theories, and developing research methods. Whereas media studies generally refutes the idea of an "epistemic thing" altogether and celebrates a multitude of disciplinary orientations within the scientific community, gender studies can (also) be characterized by chiasms between basic and applied research that have been developed as a consequence of the historical rootedness of the discipline in a political movement. As strong as the paradigm of the performativity of gender might seem to scholars from all disciplinary settings of gender studies, this becomes more strategic upon closer inspection. Artistic research is transdisciplinary in a different way: whereas a definition of the epistemic quality of artistic research might be a stronghold of its disciplinary nature, the research projects usually entail transgressions of art disciplines, maybe also part of the heritage of conceptualism.

I wanted to show that the mainstream use of transdisciplinarity as a *sine qua non* for academic thinking does not make much sense. If the term "transdisciplinarity" needs to be understood as a phenomenon dependent on the respective disciplinary context within which it is conceptualized, historically developed, and so forth, the term can hardly have a meaning beyond the signifier of an outmoded fashion. I will stick with Foucault, not only because this is usually a good idea, but also because I believe that if we understand the transgression of a border as the operation that brings the border to materialization, we have a very important analytical tool at our disposal—as opposed to a label that sells project proposals, program documents, and RTI strategies.[19]

Literature

Baldauf, Anette, and Ana Hoffner, "Kunst-basierte Forschung und methodischer Störsinn," in *Critical Studies. Kultur- und Sozialtheorie im Kunstfeld*, ed. Elke Gaugele and Jens Kastner, Vienna: Springer, 2015, pp. 325–338.

Braidt, Andrea B, *Film-Genus: Gender und Genre in der Filmwahrnehmung*, Marburg: Schüren, 2008.

Butler, Judith, *Bodies That Matter: On the Discursive Limits of "Sex"*, New York: Routledge, 1993.

—, *Gender Trouble: Feminism and the Subversion of Identity*. New York: Routledge, 1990.

19 RTI is the acronym for Research, Technology and Innovation.

Deuber-Mankowsky, Astrid, “Gender – Ein Epistemisches Ding? Zur Geschichtlichkeit Des Verhältnisses Von Natur, Kultur, Technik Und Geschlecht.” in *Was kommt nach der Genderforschung? Zur Zukunft der Feministischen Theoriebildung*, ed. Rita Casale and Barbara Rendtorff, Bielefeld: transcript, 2008, pp. 169–90.

Feyerabend, Paul, *Wider den Methodenzwang*, Frankfurt am Main: Suhrkamp, 1976.

Foucault, Michel, “Zum Begriff der Übertretung,” trans. Karin von Hofer, in *Schriften zur Literatur*, ed. TKTK, Munich: Nymphenburger Verlagshandlung, 1974, pp. 69–87.

Kuhn, Thomas S, *Die Struktur wissenschaftlicher Revolutionen* (1962), trans. Hermann Vetter, 2nd ed., Frankfurt am Main: Suhrkamp, 1976.

Pias, Claus (ed.), *Was waren Medien?* Zurich: diaphanes, 2010.

Rheinberger, Hans-Jörg, *Experimentalsysteme und epistemische Dinge: Eine Geschichte der Proteinsynthese im Reagenzglas*, Frankfurt am Main: Suhrkamp, 2006.

Scheele, Brigitte and Norbert Groeben, *Die Heidelberger Struktur-Lege-Technik (Slt): Eine Dialog-Konsens-Methode zur Erhebung subjektiver Theorien mittlerer Reichweite* [Beiheft Zum Legekasten], Weinheim, Basel: Beltz Verlag, 1984.

Schiesser, Giaco, “What Is at Stake? Qu’est-ce que l’enjeu? Paradoxes, Problematics, Perspectives in Artistic Research Today,” in *Art, Research, Innovation and Society*, ed. Gerald Bast and Elias G. Carayannis, Vienna: Springer, 2015, p. 96.

Scott, Joan W., “Gender: A Useful Category for Historical Analysis,” *American Historical Review* 91, no. 5 (December 1986), pp. 1053–1075.

Marco Meier

Response to Andrea B. Braidt

Thank you very much for your presentation. I may be, more or less, the ideal person to make a response to your talk, having passed most of my active life in the media—print, radio, and TV. I've never—until hearing your talk—connected the direct genealogy of gender studies to media studies and artistic research. I think it's really a good and proper approach. I especially like the aspects of mimetic thinking and the clarity of reaction in a normative and political sense. I appreciate this, because you present a dimension and an inclusion that we all might think to be obvious, and as we discussed with Professor Sabine Maasen before: why is something that seems to be methodologically obvious so often absent from scholarly work and scientific research in practice? I realize or ask myself how difficult it must be for a young scientist to choose a transdisciplinary subject of research and to finally realize, whilst leaving the ordinary disciplinary mainstream, that he or she might lose the chance of official recognition, for lack of possibilities to publish, including the difficulty of getting funding for a transdisciplinary project.

Having said that, I would have liked to change to German, my mother tongue. Why would I have preferred to do so? (Well, let's continue in English.) One of my first workshops at the Collegium Helveticum some years ago was about "Sprachenvielfalt", the diversity of languages. And I remember the vivid discussions about the ambivalence of English as the new "lingua franca." We discussed the importance not only of using our native language in a local but also in a scientific context. In fact, every discipline has by nature its very own, special scientific language. And if we really want to be transdisciplinary in the original sense, we have to accept the diversity of languages as a primary source of transgression. And by the way, here in this very building we host the famous Ludwik-Fleck-Center. Ludwik Fleck considered the importance of a genuine "Denkstil" and "Denkkollektiv" in every scientific community.

I believe, to a certain extent, that we find ourselves in a particularly European discussion, which shows us how English as a "universal language" might lead to a drastic reduction of discursive diversity. No one doubts the global importance of English in political and scientific understanding. Nobody wants to turn back this universal dimension of scientific exchange. A sophisticated, international, scientific institution wouldn't stand a chance by being nationally protectionist. However, English as a unified language can indeed appear to be reductionist. Interdisciplinary exchange especially requires a transcending, linguistic communicative sensibility in its translation. To mention Fleck again, it's about respect for the language and its particular culture of thought. This is only a small, incidental remark in a wider field of communicative diversity. In the end it's about cultural and linguistic resistance. It's become evident that since Brexit and the election of Donald Trump as president of the US, that the voices of protectionism are coming mainly from the Anglo-Saxon world.

This brings us immediately to current political events. We have just witnessed a phenomenon which, following Professor Andrea Braidt's remarks, took us by surprise on three levels: the media, the gender question, and the artistic mimesis. Donald Trump's election is an exemplary reflection on the efficacy of a media, a gender-specific, and an artistic performance, in this specific case, resulting in an interpretive calamity. Political commentators, poll-takers, and the media did not expect that the real estate mogul would ever have had the slightest chance of winning the US presidential election.

No one in my circle of friends considered getting up at 3 a.m. to watch the three live debates between Hillary Clinton and Donald Trump. But I did, not exactly knowing why. It was definitely not because of insomnia. It was more of an intuition than a clear intention. I vaguely remembered three events in the 1970s that lured us to the TV sets at about the same time in the morning. They were the live broadcasts of the legendary boxing matches between Muhammad Ali, alias Cassius Clay and, if I remember correctly, Sonny Liston, Floyd Patterson, and Joe Frazier. The US pop culture celebrated here a paradigmatic media and macho-gender event, as well as an artistic performance at its best. A star, seen around the globe, synchronized via the "hot technology" of television, was born. My memory of these events is black and white.

And now, 40 years later, the live broadcasts of the duel between the Democrat Hillary Clinton and the Republican Donald Trump. Of course, I could not have dared to predict Trump's victory. He was rhetorically much worse than Hillary Clinton. He seemed uninformed, contradicted himself often, was tense and frequently verbally abusive. Yet somehow, one felt that something extraordinary was happening in front of the TV cameras, eerily undermining a complete set of rules in the game of public political discourse. A disruptive re-interpretation was underway that asymmetrically played against any established form of communication. These were the forerunners of a total semiotic confusion. Was this satire, or a reality show, or a genuine political event? Or everything together, in a singular transmedia mix?

Andrea Braidt, in her lecture, quoted Michel Foucault from his famous text "A Preface to Transgression": "Transgression forces the limit to face the fact of its imminent disappearance, to find itself in what it excludes (perhaps, to be more exact, to recognize itself for the first time), to experience its positive truth in its downward fall."

Professor Braidt presented us, in an enlightened, epistemological attempt, with an analysis of the transdisciplinary approach in gender studies, media studies and arts research.

Foucault's narrative of transgression thus becomes an emancipatory moment of normative-critical competence. In the supremely precarious and fragile transitions between the different researched environments, for a short moment one touches on appearance and disappearance, the epistemology of a genuine fragment of truth.

Donald Trump didn't read his Foucault. But his confusing mass-media game is anything but harmless. One might presume, with some degree of probability, that his consultant, Steve Bannon, is behind this vile yet obviously effective attentiveness- and visibility-management, which, with all the available means of populist seduction, flutters between all realities of the mass media with apparent agility. In their contorted guise, Andrea Braidt's citation of Judith Butler's theses about performativity seem to oscillate in a militantly obstructive intention to circumvent the concerns of the gender discourse. Trump's election-campaign rhetoric against Hillary Clinton ran on a calculated sexist narrative.

Why am I making this link between the media events concerning the US presidential elections and the theory of a mandatory transdisciplinary transgression of common domains in research brought forward by Andrea Braidt? One cannot counter this approach with an enlightened and critical intention. The Trump media phenomenon, however, clearly shows that this transgressive moment, in times of increasingly limitless and ever faster moving digital media dynamics, reveals a structure of normative arbitrariness that makes the good old search for truth only conditionally favorable. "Fake news," "alternative facts," and "social bots" are warning signs in today's politics, which use transgression as a principle, in order to address the populace and tell them exactly what they want to hear.

I understand Braidt's lecture, as an appeal for transdisciplinary vigilance in regard to gender, the media and the arts. It will be crucial to find the proper methodological instruments in order to read the signs of our times in due course.

Transdisciplinary links (crossings/transgressions) are only epistemologically productive when being experienced as such. A semiotic disorientation would follow if they became instrumentally blurred or deliberately looped.

The general weather situation, in its solipsistic echo chambers, threatens to reduce the cultural room for interpretation into a black hole of instant communication. This would undoubtedly mean the end of semiotics. The transitions between media and technology corporations would become the norm, corresponding with the credo of the Silicon Valley hippie capitalists in any case. The space-time dimension as a precondition and possibility of whichever interpretation would be sacrificed for the purely functional logic of algorithms. This would then take on the form of a "condensed experience," thus in complete contradiction to what Andrea Braidt calls "epistological potential." It is all the more apparent to agree with her claim: "What the discourse about transgressing disciplinary borders needs is differentiation." And it is a wish for the media sciences to pay more attention to the "epistemic thing." Their proverbial "lack of discipline" threatens to become a political boomerang.

Sabine Maasen

Collaborating In and Beyond Science

Obstacles and (Somewhat Surprising) Opportunities

The never-ending quest for collaboration

The idea that single disciplines may not be enough for studying, understanding, or even solving problems at hand, is not new at all. It all began with the notion of interdisciplinarity, and has been promoted by several movements. A brief sketch of the story of interdisciplinarity may tell that the urge to go beyond the scope of disciplines is part and parcel of reflecting on science since the 20th century (for the following, see also Weingart 2000, pp. 25–41).

One of these movements is called the Unity of Science. It campaigned in the 1930s and 40s, one important group being the Vienna Circle. It sought a common empirical attitude toward all the sciences, and strove to develop a single, comprehensive scientific language. This endeavor has been dismissed as utterly reductionist, as different disciplines did not collaborate with each other but were reduced to a single basic scientific discipline, namely physics. In this tradition the concept of interdisciplinarity was driven by mainly epistemic interests for some time.

Things only changed in the 1960s. The call for interdisciplinarity gained a second momentum in the US and Europe with the student unrests in the late 1960s. Here it began to enter the political arena. One of the demands was for disciplinary structures in universities to be replaced by more holistic concepts that were closer to practical life. Political circles also became enthused by planning on the basis of scientific knowledge (particularly in the realm of education). In this context, interdisciplinarity came to denote reform, innovation, and progress way beyond academia (Weingart and Stehr 2000). In 1972, after extensive cross-national research, the OECD published its seminal volume on *Interdisciplinarity*, designed to promote interdisciplinarity in teaching and university organizational structures. Several studies and conferences followed. However, when the OECD published *Interdisciplinarity Revisited* a decade and a half later, the sobering result was that interdisciplinarity had lost its momentum and the disciplines had in fact been strengthened again.

In the course of the 1990s, interdisciplinarity came to be associated with yet another trend, namely with the label "knowledge society." The observation was that science and society were moving ever closer to one another. Virtually every domain of society was realized to be suffused by science and technology, constantly challenging society and its members. Accordingly, research needed to be directed toward effectiveness and relevance. "New modes of knowledge production" were called for (Gibbons et al. 1994). These and other concepts maintained, among other things, that research had to meet novel requirements: next to being epistemically sound, it had to be economically profitable, politically relevant, and socially robust. Notably, it had to be problem-oriented and targeted at solutions rather than playing academic glass bead games.

From the 1990s onwards the prime condition and goal for interdisciplinarity was therefore its contribution to governing contemporary society by relevant scientific and technological knowledge. At this point in time we start talking about transdisciplinarity. As Jürgen Mittelstrass puts it: "Transdisciplinarity is a form of scientific work which arises in cases concerning the solution of non-scientific problems, for instance the above-mentioned environmental, energy and health care policy problems, as well as an intrascientific principle concerning the order of scientific knowledge and scientific research itself. In both cases, transdisciplinarity is a principle of research and science, one which becomes operative wherever it is impossible to define or attempt to solve problems within the boundaries of subjects or disciplines, or where one goes beyond such definitions" (Mittelstrass 2011, p. 331).

When it comes to present-day knowledge politics, there is no doubt about it, interdisciplinarity, and more specifically transdisciplinarity, are the most popular catchwords. In actual fact they are often used interchangeably, the reason presumably being that they are united by a common appeal: both terms carry the idea of effectively countering over-specialization in research, development, and teaching. On the other hand they carry the hope for more effectively dealing with issues that are regarded as too complex to be dealt with by one field of expertise only.

This is also mirrored in the politics of funding agencies. Prior to 1980 they spoke in the name of science to the nation states, articulating the needs of science. After 1980 funding agencies begin to speak to science, urging reforms and increased cooperation among scientists and beyond (Kwa 2006). Funding schemes today not only govern the choice of topics, agendas, methods, etc., but also the early dissemination of outcomes and the ongoing networking activities of all stakeholders.

At the peak of this trend, the "grand challenges" have appeared: they too address problems such as climate change or energy security, yet from now on at a global scale, and they call for nothing less than novel approaches and technical solutions. As of 2000 this sets the stage for interdisciplinarity anew: in EU parlance, transdisciplinarity is now reframed as "science in society, with society, for society." In its research and innovation framework program Horizon 2020, for instance, the European Union posits that collaboration across sciences, social sciences, arts, and humanities, is the source of "radical breakthroughs with a transformative impact" (European Commission 2011, p. 35), and in Germany the Deutsche Forschungsgemeinschaft (DFG) states in its institutional mission that they address challenges such as "the interdisciplinarisation of the sciences and humanities" (DFG 2015).

Despite this overwhelming rhetoric, virtually nobody denies transdisciplinary collaboration to be easier said than done.[1] Why, then, can't we leave it at that? There are at least two reasons why not: Politically speaking, collaboration in and beyond academia is strongly linked to innovation. Normatively speaking, it is supposed to be inclusive as it exploits a wider knowledge base and involves a broader set of stakeholders. As a consequence, transdisciplinarity is as politically overdetermined (solutions for problems) as it is epistemically underdetermined (see below).

Given the above, how can one make sense of these contradictory messages? While the literature on interdisciplinarity has focused on typologies and taxonomies (Barry et al. 2008; Klein 2010a), as well as on how particular (inter)disciplines (Abbott 2001; Holmwood 2010; Schoolman et al. 2012; Jasanoff 2013) and specific projects (Rabinow and Bennett 2012; Centellas et al. 2014) work, the prevalence of ambivalent rhetoric attached to collaboration has often been overlooked. According to a recent study by Cuevas Garcia, interdisciplinarity is alternatively seen

1 In the UK, in the years before the last Research Excellence Framework (REF), several academics claimed in newspapers and blogs that, contrary to the research councils, such an evaluation exercise discourages interdisciplinary research. Moreover, as physicist Athene Donald wrote on her blog: "Spreading one's wings into [...] pastures new has to be good for all kinds of reasons beyond simply the CV and the next job application. But, go too far and it is of course possible that glib superficiality will set in." (Donald 2015)

as an intellectual bonus, or as non-rigorous; as rewarding in itself, or as an intellectual challenge; as an institutional desire, or as an institutional challenge, which is problematic because institutional support is fundamental for interdisciplinarity. While it can be seen as an instrumental bonus, it can also be seen as purely instrumental rather than authentic, and as precarious (Cuevas-Garcia 2017, p. 17).

At the same time, the quest for collaboration abounds with strong unifying ambitions such as "joint goals" and "shared values" and, last but not least, "consensus." This, however, is neither the rationale nor the practice of collaboration. Rather, disciplines or fields are characterized by differences and by boundaries: we cooperate because we differ in our notions and values. The different factions working together, say scientists of various disciplines, industrial actors and concerned citizens, typically do not share their views when starting their cooperation, and chances are that they won't share it after their cooperation. But maybe they will come to know the reasons for their differences in perspective, and find out about a new way to frame a problem so as to proceed despite the differences that will remain. The magic formula being: informed dissent. In this view, transdisciplinarity is all about working with differences and boundaries between disciplines, stakeholders, organizations, and values. The ultimate trick for collaboration to happen is to engineer socio-intellectual spaces that allow for trading differences, and dissent even, in a productive way.

In order to substantiate my claim, let me begin by a closer look at collaborative practice and its value proposition. Second, I'd like to talk about the obstacles to collaboration, third the emergence of team science to improve collaborative expertise. Fourth, I would like to elaborate on the role of boundaries for collaboration. Fifth, I will approach collaboration with the help of concepts from my home turf, science and technology studies (STS). Ultimately, and with a non-provocative intention, I will plead for "idiocy" to play a decisive role in interdisciplinarity.

Collaborative practice and its forms and value propositions

For a start, let us briefly remind ourselves of the value proposition of interdisciplinarity in different domains, such as problem-solving, commercial development of a new product, or in science (Blackwell et al. 2009, p. 10):

- In academic, curiosity-driven research the main objective is directed towards new insights created by the new conjunction of differing interests and perspectives. Different disciplines combine in ways that may stimulate breakthroughs. Such research may eventually result in breakthrough opportunities for later commercial application, or as foundations for innovative cultural and social action, yet this is not the primary objective.
- In the areas of problem-solving or of the commercial development of a new product, service, or process, the objectives may be tightly defined. Here interdisciplinarity is meant to make use of different skills or analytic perspectives—to frame the problem or opportunity, to bring to bear different kinds of knowledge so as to achieve a richer solution. The belief is that interdisciplinarity increases the likelihood of a radical solution to the problem or to achieving commercialization of the opportunity.

Next to these different value propositions of collaboration in different domains and for different purposes, we should also talk about the different types of collaborative research. Since about the 1990s, it has become customary to differentiate at least three (ideal) types of collaborative work within and beyond science:

Collaborative research encompasses different degrees of cooperation, using the analogy of the ladder of participation in participatory or action research (Arnstein 1969).

- *Cross-disciplinarity* describes the loosest and least specific form of collaboration among disciplines, involving or linking two or more scientific disciplines typically, without a closer description of the purpose and the methodology of the involvement.
- *Multidisciplinarity* is more intense in the sense that multidisciplinary research has a clear purpose of joint problem-solving by involving different disciplines. Multidisciplinary research works on different aspects of a problem in parallel, is more often temporary, and is limited to a specific project or problem.
- *Interdisciplinarity* entails the most intense collaboration, involving the dissolution of disciplinary boundaries, from the problem definition to the methodology. Our understanding of interdisciplinarity follows the definition by Repko et al., who review several widely used definitions of interdisciplinary research, extract their common elements and finally condense them into the following: "Interdisciplinary studies is a process of answering a question, solving a problem or addressing a topic that is too broad or complex to be dealt with adequately by a single discipline, and draws on the disciplines with the goal of integrating their insights to construct a more comprehensive understanding" (Repko et al. 2011, p. 25).
- *Transdisciplinarity* is defined as the cooperation between scientists in academia on the one hand, and practitioners, decision makers, or the public at large on the other, and is not examined in this study. Nonetheless it is important to provide our definition of the term to distinguish it from the others mentioned above, particularly as it is used synonymously with interdisciplinarity or action research (Hirsch-Hadorn et al. 2008). In the European tradition, transdisciplinary "research takes up concrete problems of society and works out solutions through cooperation between actors and scientists" (Häberli et al. 2001, p. 6).

When it comes to actual collaborative research and development, you will regularly find all these forms throughout the process—and, by the way, also disciplinary ones. A group may negotiate the problem and the agenda together, branch out into disciplinary working groups, then discuss interim results with stakeholders, etc. Talking about cross-, multi-, inter-, or transdisciplinary collaboration is meant to draw our attention to the fact that different kinds of collaborative activities exist, and that they vary in how they lay out, understand and actually work with different kinds of knowledge and values. In this perspective, transdisciplinarity is the most demanding form of cooperation as it calls for the interaction of different disciplines, organizations, sets of knowledge, and values.

Given the focus on both economic innovation and societal acceptance today, we increasingly engage in transdisciplinary interactions such as between scientists, engineers, citizens, policy makers, and managers. Indeed, for those who are committed to solving complex social-technical problems, collaboration among diverse stakeholders is key (Cundill et al. 2015). Transdisciplinary research makes science and decision-making interactive through the coproduction of knowledge with society (Max-Neef 2005), and success is often deemed to be a function of the degree to which science, management, planning, policy, and practice are interactively involved in issue-framing, knowledge production, and knowledge application (Reyers et al. 2010; Roux et al. 2010).

Obstacles to collaborative practices

At this point, the question arises as to whether and how collaboration is, in fact, doable. And this is an important question, for there *are* considerable obstacles when it comes to practicing collaborative activity in science. Among the most imminent obstacles to interdisciplinarity we find epistemological differences, different conventions regarding the collection and analysis of data, organizational aspects, and institutional conditions for pursuing interdisciplinary projects. The obstacles show even more distinctly in cooperation across epistemic cultures. Let me mention them just very briefly:

- *Epistemological aspects*: Clearly, positivist methodologies among natural scientists and constructivist methodologies among social scientists don't sit easily side by side. Moreover, while natural scientists from different disciplines may cooperate on the basis of their positivist methodologies, cooperation among the multiparadigmatic social sciences seems less convenient. In addition, both camps prefer different research designs (i.e. experimental versus explorative).
- *Different research conventions*: Disciplines, notably those belonging to different cultures, also differ in their views on how research is done properly: this pertains, among other things, to the duration of data collection and analysis, to different levels of analysis, to different ways of communicating results, as well as to different "jargons." Particularly tricky, however, are terms that are seemingly shared by all members of an interdisciplinary team yet differ as to their meaning. Examples are "code," "information," or "model."
- *Organizing interdisciplinary teams* is a very demanding task. Coordinating schedules of team members, moderating team meetings via various media (email, Skype, etc.) requires time and staff. In this dimension, the main obstacles show in the difficulty of maintaining the high commitment of all involved. This is serious given that there are hardly any chances to sanction low commitment.
- *Institutional aspects*: The problem of maintaining commitment aggravates, in view of the fact that involvement in interdisciplinary programs counts as prestigious, in general, yet hardly contributes to one's reputation, especially in terms of publications. There is hardly a journal for

interdisciplinary products, let alone such that are listed in the (Social) Science Citation Index. Equally thorny is the question of whether or not young researchers should engage in interdisciplinary activities, as they are time-consuming and risky when it comes to finding an academic post.

Allow me to terminate this list of obstacles at this point. It is easy to imagine that the collaboration beyond the realm of science is also haunted by many more differences and boundaries—I will return to this point later.

Team science: on fixing the obstacles!

Given all these obstacles, on the one hand, and research questions becoming increasingly complex and thus requiring joint forces, on the other, we seem to be in need of expertise as regarding transdisciplinarity. Next to an abundance of anecdotal evidence and best practice recommendations, a whole new branch called *team science* has emerged in order to analyze and improve collaborative activities. Today, notably policy makers and major funders are pushing scientists to collaborate across disciplines, institutions, and even nations under the new banner of *team science*.

"The emerging field of the Science of Team Science (SciTS) encompasses both conceptual and methodological strategies aimed at understanding and enhancing the processes and outcomes of collaborative, team-based research" (Falk-Krzesinski et al. 2010, p. 263). Topics addressed by team science include definitions and models of team science; measurement and evaluation of team science; disciplinary dynamics and team science; structure and context for teams; institutional support and professional development for teams; management and organization for teams; and characteristics and dynamics of teams. Team science is based on multiple methods, quantitative and qualitative ones, and mostly relies on psychological and managerial theories and concepts.

By way of an example, through analysis of in-depth interviews with members of highly successful research teams and others who did not meet their goals or ended because of conflicts, Bennet & Gadlin (2012) identified key elements that seem critical for team success and effectiveness. Among the most important of these is trust: without trust, the team dynamic runs the risk of deteriorating over time. Other critical factors include developing a shared vision, strategically identifying team members and purposefully building the team, promoting disagreement while containing conflict, and setting clear expectations for sharing credit and authorship. Moreover, self-awareness and strong communication skills contribute greatly to the effective leadership and management strategies of scientific teams. While all successful teams share the characteristic of effectively carrying out these activities, there is no single formula for execution with every leader exemplifying different strengths and weaknesses. Successful scientific collaborations have strong leaders who are self-aware and are mindful of the many elements critical for supporting the science at the center of the effort.

Who would deny these findings? But somehow they seem to “manage” the issue of doing collaboration rather than taking the above-mentioned obstacles seriously. Team science, so it seems, is but a new word for an old challenge called cooperating within and beyond science despite all the different perspectives involved—differences that need to be bridged in a short time, in a problem-solving manner, and attractively for all involved. “Attractive” meaning, for example, “reputable” for the different disciplines involved, “innovative” for the industrial actors, “legitimacy-raising” for the political actors, “sustainable” for the ecologically-minded citizens. In view of these ambitions, the new field of the science of team science promises to shed light on what makes effective teams in order to produce the best outcomes.

As opposed to this rather managerial approach, and in full acknowledgement of the obstacles mentioned above, I plead for a different take on collaborative science. Ultimately it is all about *acknowledging boundaries* and it is about doing *boundary work*. This calls for a richer notion of boundaries first.

About the role of boundaries

Knowledge is developed within communities or organizations that are "bounded" in some way or another. Boundaries separate one institution from another, one discipline from another, government departments from companies, NGOs from political parties, research and development from manufacturing. Organizations and communities each rely on, and are sustained, by common, yet always specific, bodies of knowledge. Boundaries cut across our attempts to cooperate, and need not to be bypassed but rather to be addressed (Blackwell et al. 2009, p. 101ff).

Indeed, although *disciplinary boundaries* are often described as "barriers" to collaboration, they are also essential as they do not simply contain a particular set of facts, or methods or theories. Rather, they are about a certain epistemic culture; about the organization and transmission of knowledge, including a deep-rooted notion of *what is relevant* and *how things should be done*. This is what Ludwik Fleck would have termed specific thought styles characteristic of specific thought collectives.

This continues with *organizational boundaries*: doing collaborative work in academia, industry, government research or NGOs shapes individual values and intellectual styles, in a way that is preserved even as a person moves between sectors, or between organizations and disciplines. It is thus important to recognize that these different organizations have different cultures of knowledge—knowledge that is valued, bounded, and perhaps not even recognizable as knowledge when viewed from outside.

If collaborative groups are willing to accept each other's knowledge as different yet possibly useful, two things are mandatory. It is not so much about "effective communication" (thus the motto of team science) but rather about *much talking* and—as importantly—*much listening*. Collaborating groups, in this respect, are "contexts of enforced stimulation." In these contexts where heterogeneous actors, groups, or organizations meet for hours and hours, over and over again we find a lot of explaining, explaining again, arguing, reframing, experimenting and admitting that one still doesn't understand what the other person is saying. Yet by asking again, here and there, glimpses of "bridging ideas" might come up. However, more often than not, ideas, arguments, or solutions are likely

- to be different from those that were expected;
- not to be expressible in terms of the discipline or group or organization that originated the initiative;
- to involve new questions, or a reformulation of objectives;
- to arise only after a longer time—perhaps long after the initiative has formally ended.

However, there are strategies to respond to these types of outcomes. Already at the outset of collaborative endeavors, one should, for example,

- define unexpected questions as a valuable outcome;
- deliver other, more minor outcomes as "early wins" (recommended by Jeremy Baumberg);
- manage expectations by presenting the research as an attempt to produce "interesting failures."

"Valuable questions," "early wins," "interesting failures" are strategies to deal with differences and boundaries. Another important strategy is to look for shared objects, such as sketches, prototypes, or concepts. They help as a focus around which to articulate developing innovative perspectives. They also act to build trust among external stakeholders, for a concrete artifact confers validity by its very existence. A major obstacle to many interdisciplinary endeavors is that their objectives are otherwise not expressible within the value system of one or more of the contributing disciplines or organizations.

Collaborative practice according to concepts from STS

These ideas and strategies, if only mentioned by way of example, strongly rely on notions from my home discipline of science and technology studies (STS). Among many other things, STS is interested in understanding and shaping the empirical practices of doing collaboration within and beyond science. Among the most prominent concepts are the notions of "boundary objects," "trading zones," interactional expertise," and "community of practice." Let's consider them step by step.

Joint concepts, real-world problems, or prototypes are perfect examples of so-called boundary objects suggested by Susan Leigh Star and James R. Griesemer (1989). By definition, "boundary objects are both plastic enough to adapt to local needs and constraints of the several parties employing them, yet robust enough to maintain a common identity across sites. [...] They have different meanings in different social worlds but their structure is common enough to more than one world to make them recognizable, a means of translation. The creation and management of boundary objects is key in developing and maintaining coherence across intersecting social worlds."

Star and Griesemer, in their study, are concerned with the problem of how members of different social worlds (such as science, industry, and NGOs), manage to cooperate successfully. Cooperation, they argue, is necessary to ensure reliability across domains, and to gather information which retains integrity across time, space, and local contingencies. But, and this is important, it does not require consensus or unity. The boundary object in their study is the Museum of Vertebrate Zoology, whose institutionalization involved actors as different as university administrators, amateur collectors, farmers, philanthropists, and their specific interests. On my reading of Star and Griesemer's account, a boundary object is both a product and a facilitator of the multiple interactions needed to engineer productive cooperation among multiple social worlds, despite all the remaining differences in perspective.

The empirical observation is that in the course of interacting, collaborative groups often manage a kind of "trading zone" (Galison 1997, p. 783) in which the various subcultures, each with its own language, develop a "joint language," "and some experts even learn to use the language of another research community in ways that are indistinguishable from expert practitioners of that community" (Collins & Evans 2002). Galison presents the interactions of experimenters and theoreticians in terms of the "trading zones" described by anthropologists, who have extensively studied how different groups, with radically different views of the world, can not only exchange goods but also depend essentially on trading them. Analogously, within a certain arena defined by a problem or a task, two or more dissimilar groups can find common ground and trade as yet unknown, possibly complementary or opposing views, concepts, methods, "worked out in exquisite local detail, without global agreement"—just for this particular problem at hand (Galison 1997, p. 46; Thagard 2005, p. 318). A trading zone is at the same time necessary for all factions involved without the necessity of overall consensus.

The ability to converse expertly in more than one discipline is called "interactional expertise" (Collins et al. 2002). For example, somebody doing STS research on physics without actually practicing physics may acquire interactional expertise. Interactional expertise is developed through interaction without expert knowledge or practical immersion in a (slightly) foreign scientific domain. To be sure, this is not exceptional in science, but rather a regular occurrence: scientific practice requires all of us to develop such expertise, for interactional expertise is the medium of, say, "communication in peer review in science, in review committees, in interdisciplinary projects, and in the public understanding of science. It is also the medium of specialist journalists and interpretative methods in the social sciences." (Collins et al. 2002) Beyond specialist expertise in the particular field we evaluate or communicate, we create closeness and credibility for judgement by "diving into" the other field.

To sum up: a trading zone can gradually become a new area of expertise, facilitated by interactional expertise and involving negotiations over boundary objects (objects represented in different ways by different participants). If this happens, we see a collectivity emerging that is not a scientific community, yet neither is it an arbitrary collectivity any more. Rather, a "community of practice" emerges that is characterized by three interrelated concepts: "mutual engagement," "joint enterprise," and "shared repertoire" (Wenger 1988, pp. 72–73).

- Via *mutual engagement*, trading partners establish norms and build collaborative relationships;
- by *joint enterprise*, they create a domain that binds them together;
- finally, as part of its practice, the community produces a set of communal resources or a *shared repertoire*.

Viewed from the perspective of these concepts, collaborative enterprises can both acknowledge and capitalize on differences in epistemic, normative, or organizational culture. What they essentially do is engineer a socio-intellectual space around a certain problem—be it primarily academic, technical, economic, or social in nature—by trading their respective concepts or instruments, thereby building up boundary objects that, in turn, facilitate the development of interactional expertise. In the course of this happening, communities of practice emerge.

More often than not, however, inter- or transdisciplinary endeavors are temporary ones; they always convene a specific set of partners, targeting a particular problem (for instance, I did collaborative work on free will with neuroscientists, criminologists, philosophers; on the social foundations of nature with biologists, geneticists, sociobiologists, historians of science and anthropologists, and I'm planning another project on care robotics with roboticists, neuroengineers, care givers and patients). Given all these specificities, can one thus possibly become an expert in collaboration? I think so: after some practice in *engineering trading zones* one can indeed acquire a collaborative expertise in its own right that might be applied to various constellations and problems.

And the quintessential trick is: allow idiocy to play a decisive role!

Given that we deal not only with differences in knowledge but also as regards power (reputation, political status etc.), collaboration may differ considerably. MacMynowsky (2007) distinguishes four scenarios:

- *Conflict*: research might start with an interdisciplinary intent, but researchers go their separate ways.
- *Tolerant ambivalence*: researchers from different disciplines can amicably coexist, even contribute to the same project, but their analytical domains are largely separate.
- *Mutual identification and cooperation*: there are theories and analytical tools that can be transferred if effort is put into communication, consistency of models and concepts, and crossover applications of theory.

- *Fundamental reorientation and recombination of knowledge claims.*

I agree with MacMynowsky that in collaborative practice, too, knowledge mixes with power. By way of one example only, let's consider collaboration among biophysical and social scientists. "They are not just bringing information and different understandings of biophysical and social systems with them. Those knowledge claims have differential power associated with them: within the sciences, between social and biophysical sciences, and between science and society." (MacMynowsky 2007, p. 20). In the science and technology studies literature, this leads to novel insights. First, the diversity of approaches to research and the types of knowledge claims that result are often neglected and unduly homogenized (Pedynowski 2003). Second, more often than not, (trans-)academic debates have many actors with different claims and different levels of social power (Lahsen 2005).

Consequently, in view of differential power/knowledge (Foucault 1980), "the choice is whether to recognize the situation and deal with the implications as transparently, methodically, and consciously as possible, or to deny this aspect of the interdisciplinary interface and let these forces operate behind a screen of tradition, assumptions, and unexplicated values" (MacMynowsky 2007, p. 20). Chances are thus slim that we ever arrive at scenario four.

Yet there is hope—*if* we allow idiocy to play a role. In her "Cosmopolitical Proposal," Isabelle Stengers (2005) uses the figure of the idiot to think about the political consequences and challenges of slowing down thinking and decision-making, the role model being the childlike prince depicted by Fyodor Dostoevsky in his novel *The Idiot* (1868/69). Lev Myshkin does not understand conventions, assumptions, norms, jokes, metaphors. Ultimately, he does not understand the shared values of the society to which he has returned after four years abroad. He embarrasses himself, asks ridiculous questions, holds strange positions, has unfounded prejudices, etc.

How does this relate to politics, which since ancient Greece has been defined as the opposite of idiocy: with idiots one cannot talk, argue, or build a common world. Except, perhaps, in Dostoevsky's novel, in which some characters take the idiot and his views seriously. The result is a slowing down of thought and action, and with that an *opening toward the unknown*, toward *alternative definitions* of the common world.

How does the figure of the idiot help with rethinking collaborative practices? Michel Callon, Pierre Lascoumes and Yannick Barthe (2009), for instance, conceive of so-called hybrid forums as instances in which heterogeneous actors engage in the collaborative exploration of sociotechnical issues and the making of non-definitive decisions. Hybrid forums deliberately aim to accelerate the slowing down of thinking and action (Farias 2017).

Modeled after Dostoevsky, the idiot thus allows us to slow down—to take time to question our own assumptions about a problem and to reinterpret it. Following this idea, the idiotic boundary object, for instance, affords an opportunity to engage in a process of "inventive problem making" (Fraser 2010). As a methodology, the proactive idiocy is not so much about problems or facts, but about the emergence of new relations that may reconfigure what the very "fact" or "problem" might be. Fraser goes on to note that in Deleuzian terms the constitutive elements of a collaborative event or process do not simply "interact," but change in the process of that interaction, not least the researchers themselves. "In such an eventuation, researchers can now begin to query what they are 'busy doing' and imagine that there is 'something more important,' or in Fraser's articulation of the Deleuzian event, begin to move beyond finding a 'solution' to a (formally) familiar 'emergency' (of democratic deficit, say) to 'inventive problem making' in which the parameters of the issue are reconfigured" (Michael 2012, p. 535).

So in collaborative settings, the sheer presence of different sets of knowledge and values thus provokes a rethinking of what each of the participants considered evident before. On this account, interdisciplinary settings are spaces to say: I don't get it, I think otherwise, please explain again, let's try it differently—over and over again. And precisely for this reason, engineering collaboration as an idiotic practice needs nerves and courage and trust. It remains, interactional expertise notwithstanding, an ongoing experiment. Following Ignacio Farias, such experiments have to be catalyzed. They do not just happen; they have to be actively pursued (Farias 2017, p. 40). Idiocy is not just a figure; is a constitutive practice and capacity, necessary to *engineering trading zones*.

On a final note, collaboration—even more so, when it allows for idiotic practices—requires one important resource in order to achieve accountability: trust. Therefore, in collaborative research the role of trust needs be made transparent. A first step has been taken recently by several science journals, including, for example, all journals from the *Nature* group, which since 2009 has required that articles contain a contribution statement that specifies the contribution of every author (*Nature* editors 2007). As a second step, collaborators need to consider their warrant for believing in the epistemic and moral character of each of their collaborators. An initial move in this direction can be found in the so-called Vancouver Guidelines of 2013, a set of recommendations on journal publication issued by the International Committee of Medical Journal Editors (ICMJE). They specify that "authors should have confidence in the integrity of the contributions of their co-authors" (ICMJE 2014, p. 2).

However, given the afore mentioned analysis, and increasingly finely grained guidelines and statements notwithstanding, calibration of trust in collaborative practices is bound to remain a delicate task. For collaboration in and beyond academia means acknowledging boundaries and differences, so we don't competently evaluate each other's expertise but trust in it. Moreover, we have to trust in the value added by proceeding "idiotically." Why not give it a try?

References

Abbott, Andrew, *Chaos of Disciplines*, Chicago: University of Chicago Press, 2016.

Andersen, Hanne, "Collaboration, Interdisciplinarity, and the Epistemology of Contemporary Science," in *Studies in History and Philosophy of Science Part A*, no. 56 (2016), pp. 1–10.

Arnstein, Sherry R, "A Ladder of Citizen Participation," in *Journal of the American Institute of Planners* 35, no. 4 (1969), pp. 216–224.

Barry, Andrew, Georgina Born, and Gisa Weszkalnys, "Logics of Interdisciplinarity," in *Economy and Society* 37, no. 1 (2008), pp. 20–49.

Blackwell, Alan et al. *Radical Innovation: Crossing Knowledge Boundaries With Interdisciplinary Teams*, Cambridge: University of Cambridge, 2009, https://www.cl.cam.ac.uk/techreports/UCAM-CL-TR-760.pdf (accessed November 2016).

Bennett, Linda M., and H. Gadlin, "Collaboration and Team Science: From Theory to Practice," in *J Investigative Medicine* 60, no.5 (2012), pp. 768–775.

Callon, Michel, Pierre Lascoumes, and Yannick Barthe, *Acting in an Uncertain World: An Essay on Technical Democracy*, trans. Graham Burchell, Cambridge, MA: MIT Press, 2009; originally published in 2001.

Collins, Harry M., and R. Evans, "The Third Wave of Science Studies," in *Social Studies of Science* 32, no. 2 (2002), pp. 235–296.

Cuevas-Garcia, Carlos Adrian, "Understanding Interdisciplinarity in its Argumentative Context: Thought and Rhetoric in the Perception of Academic Practices," in *Interdisciplinary Science Reviews* (2017), pp. 1–20.

Cundill, Georgina, Dirk J. Roux, and John N. Parker, "Nurturing communities of practice for transdisciplinary research," in *Ecology and Society* 20, no. 2 (2002), p. 22.

Centellas, Kate M. et. al., "Calibrating Translational Cancer Research: Collaboration Without Consensus in Interdisciplinary Laboratory Meetings," in *Science, Technology & Human Values* 39, no. 3 (2014), pp. 311–335.

DFG 2015, "Institutional Website," http://www.dfg.de/en/ (accessed August 19, 2015).

Donald, Athene (2015), "How Broad is Broad," http://occamstypewriter.org/athenedonald/ (accessed November 2016).

Dostoevsky, Fyodor, *The Idiot,* trans. Richard Pevear and Larissa Volokhonsky, New York: Everyman's Library, 2002; originally published in 1868–69.

European Commission 2011, "Proposal for a Regulation of the European Parliament and of the Council Establishing Horizon 2020: The Framework Programme for Research and Innovation (2014–2020)," https://ec.europa.eu/research/horizon2020/pdf/proposals/proposal_for_a_regulation_of_the_european_parliament_and_of_the_council_establishing_horizon_2020_-_the_framework_programme_for_research_and_innovation_(2014–2020).pdf (accessed November 2016).

Falk-Krzesinski, Holly et al, "Advancing the Science of Team Science," in *Clinical and Translational Science* 3, no.5 (2010), pp. 263–266.

Farias, Ignacio, "An Idiotic Catalyst. Accelerating the Slowing Down of Thinking and Action," in *Cultural Anthropology* 31, no. 1 (2017), pp. 35–41.

Foucault, Michel, *Power/Knowledge: Selected Interviews and Other Writings 1972–1977*, New York: Pantheon Books, 1980.

Fraser, Mariam M, "Facts, Ethics, and Event," in *Deleuzian Intersections in Science. Science. Technology, and Anthropology*, ed. Casper Bruun Jensen, and Kjetil Roedje, New York: Berghahn Press, 2010, pp. 57–82.

Galison, Peter, *Image & Logic: A Material Culture of Microphysics*, Chicago: The University of Chicago Press, 1997.

Gibbons, Michael et al., *The New Production of Knowledge: The Dynamics of Science and Research in Contemporary Societies*. London: Sage, 1994.

Hirsch Hadorn, Gertrude et al., *Handbook of Transdisciplinary Research*, Heidelberg: Springer Verlag, 2008.

Häberli, Rudolf et al., *Transdisciplinarity: Joint Problem Solving among Science,Technology, and Society. An Effective Way for Managing Complexity*, Basel: Birkhäuser, 2001, pp. 6–22.

Holmwood, John, "Sociology's Misfortune: Disciplines, Interdisciplinarity and the Impact of Audit Culture," in *The British Journal of Sociology* 61, no. 4 (2010), pp. 639–658.

ICMJE, "Recommendations for the Conduct, Reporting, Editing, and Publication of Scholarly Work in Medical Journals," online source (accessed 2014).

Jasanoff, Sheila, "Fields and Fallows: A Political History of STS," in *Interdisciplinarity. Reconfigurations of the Social and Natural Sciences*, ed. A. Barry, and G. Born, University of Nottingham, 2013, pp. 99–118.

Klein, Julie T, "A Taxonomy of Interdisciplinarity," in *The Oxford Handbook of Interdisciplinarity*, ed. R. Frodeman, Julie T. Klein, and Carl Mitcham, Oxford: Oxford University Press, 2010, pp. 15–30.

Kwa, Chunglin, "Interdisciplinary Research through Informal Science-Policy Interactions," in *Science & Public Policy* 10 (2006), pp. 457–467.

Lahsen, Myanna, "Technocracy, Democracy, and U.S. Climate Politics: the Need for Demarcations," in *Science, Technology, and Human Values* 30 (2005), pp. 137–169.

Levin, Lennart, and Ingemar Lind (eds.), *Interdisciplinarity Revisited. Re-Assessing the Concept in the Light of Institutional Experience*, Stockholm: LiberFörlag, 1985.

Max-Neef, Manfred A., "Foundations of Transdisciplinarity," in *Ecological Economics* 53 (2005), pp. 5–16.

MacMynowsky, Dena, "Pausing at the Brink of Interdisciplinarity: Power and Knowledge at the Meeting of Social and Biophysical Science," in *Ecology and Society* 12, no. 1 (2007), p. 20.

Michael, Mike, "What Are We Busy Doing? Engaging the Idiot," in *Science. Technology, and Human Values* 37 (2012), pp. 528–554.

Mittelstrass, Jürgen, "On Transdisciplinarity," in *Trames* 15, no. 4 (2011), pp. 329–338.

Nature editors, "Accountability of Authors," in *Nature* 450, no. 1 (2007).

Pedynowsli, Dena, "Science(s) – Which, When, and Whose? Probing the Meta-Narrative of Scientific Knowledge in the Social Construction of Nature," in *Progress in Human Geography* 27 (2003), pp. 761–778.

Rabinow, Paul and Gaymon Bennett, *Designing Human Practices. An Experiment with Synthetic Biology*, Chicago: University of Chicago Press, 2012.

Repko, Allen F., William H. Newel, and Rick Szostak, *Case Studies in Interdisciplinary Research*, Thousand Oaks: Sage, 2011.

Reyers, B. Roux et al., "Putting Conservation Plans to Work: Conservation Planning as a Transdisciplinary Process," in *Conservation Biology* 24, no. 4 (2010), pp. 957–965.

Roux, Dirk et al., "Framework for Participative Reflection in the Accomplishment of Transdisciplinary Research Programs," in *Environmental Science & Policy* 13 (2010), pp. 733–741.

Schoolman, Ethan. D. et al., "How Interdisciplinary is Sustainability Research? Analyzing the Structure of an Emerging Scientific Field," in *Sustainability Science* 7, no. 1 (2012), pp. 67–80.

Star, Susan and James Griesemer, "Institutional Ecology, 'Translational' and Boundary Objects: Amateurs and Professionals in Berkeley's Museum of Vertebrate Zoology, 1907–1939," in *Social Studies of Science* 19 (1989), pp. 387–420.

Stengers, Isabelle, "A Cosmopolitical Proposal," in *Making Things Public: Atmospheres of Democracy*, ed. Bruno Latour and Peter Weibel, Cambridge, MIT Press, 2005, pp. 994–1003.

Thagard, Paul, *Mind: Introduction to Cognitive Science*, Cambridge, MA: MIT Press, 2005.

Weingart, Peter, "Interdisciplinarity: The Paradoxical Discourse," in *Practising Interdisciplinarity*, ed. Peter Weingart and Nico Stehr, Toronto: University of Toronto Press, 2000.

Weingart, Peter and Nico Stehr, *Practising Interdisciplinarity*, Toronto: University of Toronto Press, 2000.

Wenger, Étienne, *Communities of Practice: Learning, Meaning, and Identity*, Cambridge: Cambridge University Press, 1998.

Christoph Schenker

Transdisciplinarity and Condensed Knowledge

Response to Sabine Maasen

In the following I shall reply to several aspects addressed by Sabine Maasen in her paper and relate them to the field of the fine arts. In drawing attention to artists in this context, I am referring specifically to those who conduct research just as scientists do. There is not room here to elaborate on the conditions under which artistic activity constitutes research.

In an article on public art published in 1997, the French artist Daniel Buren argued that artists must abandon the isolation of their studios and work together with other competent people in order to realize their projects.[1] Buren consistently designed his projects in and for specific contexts. In art speak this approach is known as site-specific art; he himself uses the term *in situ*. The word "context" embraces not only topological, physical, and architectural contexts but also social, political, economic, institutional, and legal ones. The circumstances involved in situations of this kind entail dealing with issues that are too complex to be handled by a single artist. For Buren, involving the expertise of others in carrying out a project also means engaging in a dialogue with the public.

1 Here and in the following see Daniel Buren, "Kann die Kunst die Straße erobern?" in Klaus Bussmann, Kasper König and Florian Matzner (eds.), *Skulptur: Projekte in Münster 1997*, Ostfildern-Ruit: Gerd Hatje, 1997, pp. 482–507.

As students at the University of Zurich in the 1980s, we were sensitized by Paul Feyerabend's unorthodox, cross-disciplinary lecture series at the neighboring Federal Institute of Technology, which also made us receptive to Helga Nowotny's academic activities here in the second half of the 1990s. We were specifically interested in her analysis of what she calls "Mode-2 knowledge production"[2]—for obvious reasons, one would think, but we did not notice the congruence until years later. In the wake of the revival and growing significance of public art, Buren referred in his article to aspects earlier described by Nowotny as the underpinnings and characteristics of Mode-2: namely, the increasing complexity and growing pressure of relevant real-world problems even as knowledge production is ever more application-oriented and site-specific, and transdisciplinarity as a privileged form of knowledge production, involving cooperation among heterogeneous agents, scientists, practitioners, and stakeholders, as well as entering into a dialogue with the public.[3] This leads to what Nowotny has described as knowledge that is reliable and socially robust.[4] She also points out the non-hierarchical and temporary nature of such cooperation, and comes to the conclusion that the relationship between sciences and society must be revised. As applied to art, Buren argues that art *extra muros*, in other words outside of art institutions with their specialized audience, cannot survive without bringing about profound changes in entrenched modes of thinking and working.

2 Michael Gibbons, Camille Limoges, Helga Nowotny, Simon Schwartzman, Peter Scott and Martin Trow, *The New Production of Knowledge: The Dynamics of Science and Research in Contemporary Societies*, London: Sage, 1994.

3 Helga Nowotny, "Transdisziplinäre Wissensproduktion: Eine Antwort auf die Wissensexplosion?" in Friedrich Stadler (ed.), *Wissenschaft als Kultur: Österreichs Beitrag zur Moderne*, Vienna: Springer, 1997, pp. 177–195.

4 Helga Nowotny, Peter Scott and Michael Gibbons, *Re-Thinking Science: Knowledge and the Public in an Age of Uncertainty*, Cambridge: Polity, 2001, pp. 166–178.

It seems to me that Sabine Maasen basically shares Nowotny's understanding of the term "transdisciplinarity."[5] Both scholars recognize that transdisciplinary practice includes not only the knowledge of different scientific disciplines but also extra-scientific knowledge and the negotiation of knowledge in public space. Their expanded understanding of the term distinguishes them from Jürgen Mittelstrass, for whom interdisciplinary and transdisciplinary practice are, if I interpret him correctly, the exclusive domain of science, even when addressing non-scientific issues.[6] Moreover, Nowotny and Maasen equally refer to the role of "trading zones" and the "boundary objects" within them[7] in describing the collaboration between actors in various disciplines and epistemic cultures. Zones of exchange and boundary objects are marked by the ambivalence of constituting the precondition for transdisciplinary processes and, conversely, of being generated by these processes to begin with. While Nowotny places Mode-2, and hence transdisciplinarity, in the context of a global explosion of knowledge, acceleration, expansion, differentiation, and the multiplication of knowledge generation,[8] Maasen, whose field is the sociology of science, directs her attention to social and work-technical aspects as well as academic and political research factors in examining the development and significance of transdisciplinarity. Nowotny places transdisciplinary work in the framework of Mode-2 knowledge production; for Maasen, the framework for transdisciplinary practices is more concretely provided by collective practices, their organization, management, engineering, and governing. Transdisciplinarity is an extremely efficient but

5 Here and in the following see Sabine Maasen, "Collaborating In and Beyond Science," in this publication.

6 Jürgen Mittelstrass, "Methodische Transdisziplinarität," in *Technikfolgenabschätzung: Theorie und Praxis*, no. 2, vol. 14, June 2005, pp. 18–23.

7 Maasen, in this publication; Nowotny et al., *Re-Thinking Science*, pp. 143–165.

8 Nowotny, "Transdisziplinäre Wissensproduktion."

also exceptionally demanding form of collaborative practice. As such, in addition to the specialist expertise of participants from various disciplines, it requires another kind of expertise, which Maasen terms "interactional expertise": the ability to be conversant in more than one discipline and to interact in the trading zones between the disciplines.

So where does art come in? I refer to art all the more emphatically inasmuch as Sabine Maasen does not mention the field as a form of knowledge when speaking of other, non-scientific disciplines within the framework of transdisciplinarity. For practicality's sake, I shall speak about our own practice: our first research project on public art, carried out in 2001/02 at the Zurich University of the Arts, was conducted by a small, interdisciplinary, largely scientific team, whose members worked in close cooperation with several artists to explore new forms of art.[9] Daniel Buren's argument served as our benchmark. Our objective was to go beyond the new forms of art that we were exploring in order to determine new, locally relevant functions of public art; to address new, explicitly contemporary subject matters and issues, and to chart new, different contexts. Specialists and the public contributed local expertise and lay knowledge; the project was also the subject of public debate. In a subsequent, much more complex and demanding project, the public sector figured more prominently as stakeholder.[10] In the third project, still underway, we are working with interdisciplinary collaboratives in nine major cities all over the world.[11] The project is an experiment in which the transdisciplinary collaboration within

9 Christoph Schenker (ed.), *Public Plaiv: Art contemporauna illa Plaiv*, Zurich: Hochschule für Gestaltung und Kunst Zürich, 2002.

10 Christoph Schenker and Michael Hiltbrunner (eds.), *Kunst und Öffentlichkeit: Kritische Praxis der Kunst im Stadtraum Zürich*, Zurich: JRP Ringier, 2007.

11 *Draft*, ongoing project since 2015, directed by Gitanjali Dang and Christoph Schenker, with collaboratives in Beijing, Cairo, Cape Town, Hamburg, Hong Kong, Mexico City, Mumbai, St. Petersburg and Zurich.

each of the teams and their respective publics has to be factored into the exchange among various cultures represented by the nine teams. To a certain extent, artists and scientists all over the world can rely on shared basic parameters. However, public art is intertwined with the political, social, and cultural environment, and impacted by local contingencies, particularities, and singularities. Whether planned and visible or accidental and veiled, trading zones or "transaction spaces"[12] emerge not only between specific disciplines but also between culturally divergent ways of life.

I refer to these examples because here in the field of public art a procedure that is self-evident though hidden in other areas of art—and not just since the end of the 20th century—has proven to be particularly fruitful. Collaborative practices in the field of the fine arts, which mean crossing the boundaries of art and the sciences, have become a widespread procedure, most especially in the field of artistic research. However, given the diversity and changing combinations of actors, who adapt to local and often short-term conditions and needs, it is often no easy task to recognize how the process of transdisciplinary collaboration is structured or organized as regards timing and communication, competencies, fields of knowledge, material realities, technologies, tools, infrastructures, and finally institutional contingencies. In addition there is a tendency to focus on the artwork itself and to mistake it for the boundary object. Actually, the work of art is a tool that the artist uses to create the—possibly immaterial—boundary object in collaboration with the other actors in the transdisciplinary process, who in turn make use of other tools. Even if the research project is conducted in the field of art, and even if a work of art is produced in the course of the project, the latter is not necessarily a boundary object or

12 Nowotny et al., *Re-Thinking Science*, pp. 143–147.

a "Mode-2 object"[13] as defined by Maasen and Nowotny—nor is it an "epistemic thing" in the sense of Hans-Jörg Rheinberger.[14]

Boundary crossing activities, in which artistic work might be involved, can also be seen from another perspective. I am not speaking here of collaboration between actors in different disciplines (including art and the public) but rather of the interplay among various forms of knowledge within the field of artistic work itself. According to Jean-François Lyotard, knowledge and science are not identical, and knowledge [*savoir*] cannot be reduced to learning [*connaisance*].[15] Lyotard juxtaposes scientific knowledge with knowledge as "training and culture," the latter characterized by a dense fabric of various competencies. These refer to thinking, making and acting, motivated not only by the criterion of truth but also by the criteria of justice and happiness (ethical wisdom), aesthetic correctness (beauty, interestingness), and efficiency (technical qualification). Lyotard uses the terms "narrative knowledge" and "condensed knowledge" when speaking of knowledge that involves not only epistemic competence but also competence and good performance in such fields as aesthetics, technology, ethics, politics, and economics. Such knowledge comprises know-how, knowing how to live, how to speak, how to listen [*savoir-faire*, *savoir-vivre*, *savoir-dire*, *savoir-écouter*], etc.

Art can also be interpreted as condensed knowledge, as a generator and form of condensed knowledge. Empirically one can observe and therefore assert, though only as a generalization, that artistic work assembles and interrelates several competencies or forms of knowledge. Art does not refer exclusively

13 Ibid, pp. 147ff.

14 Hans-Jörg Rheinberger, *Toward a History of Epistemic Things: Synthesizing Proteins in the Test Tube*, Redwood City, CA: Stanford University Press, 1997, pp. 24–37.

15 Here and in the following see Jean-François Lyotard, *The Postmodern Condition: A Report on Knowledge*, Minneapolis: University of Minnesota Press, 1984 (French 1979), pp. 18–27.

to itself, and it is not its own exclusive (re)source; it makes an impact both inside and outside of its own territory. On the one hand the artist's experimental system addresses both aesthetics and the material and technical factors involved in the making of art. This refers to the tradition of understanding works of art as aesthetic things, as objects or as instruments. On the other hand, this system refers to the tradition of problems, issues, and subject matter that lie beyond the physical production of artifacts. Making new distinctions within sensual, emotional, and intellectual experiences of violence and placelessness in the context of global capital, post-politics, and post-colonialism could, for example, be a subject of artistic research. After all, artists' explorations incorporate the common-sense practices of daily life, as applied to their own personal life experiences. Comparable to the figure of the intellectual, artists thereby move beyond the specific knowledge and competences conventionally assigned to them as artists. Strictly speaking, an artist proves to be an artist through the very act of transgressing the bounds of aesthetics.

Although I would not claim that art as a whole is a zone of exchange, a space of transaction among knowledge cultures and lifeforms with the artist as "interactional expert," I would, nonetheless, venture to say that art has assimilated transgression. Does this also account for the distinction between condensed knowledge and transdisciplinarity? I would like to put a query up for debate: namely whether there is a comparable narrative, though latent knowledge in the sciences, linked to scientific knowledge. This has undoubtedly been suggested by Hannes Rickli's artistic research into videograms of experiments in behavioural biology, which might be seen as science studies or as laboratory studies using artistic means.[16] Rickli

16 Hannes Rickli (ed.), *Videograms: The Pictorial Worlds of Biological Experimentations as an Object of Art and Theory*, Zurich: Scheidegger & Spiess, 2011.

shows scientists conducting experiments in the laboratory, in a practice and with competences that precede the scientific and are nonetheless inalienably part of it.[17]

---

17 Translation by Catherine Schelbert.

Elisabeth Bronfen

Crossmapping

A Hermeneutic Practice

When I first introduced my notion of crossmapping, in a collection of essays published under the title, *Liebestod und Femme Fatale*, in 2004, I was following an intuition.[1] Having noticed the thematic connection between a plot structure common to classic film-noir narratives and Wagner's *Tristan and Isolde*—a young man intervenes in the unhappy marriage between an older, powerful man and his dangerously alluring wife—I became curious to see if mapping a set of films from the 1940s (Jacques Tourneur's OUT OF THE PAST, Robert Siodmak's CRISS CROSS and Billy Wilder's DOUBLE INDEMNITY) onto the opera libretto would help me understand more about both the Wagnerian charting of the world and that of his cinematic successors and inheritors. In this endeavor I was guided by the conversation Stanley Cavell proposes between classic Hollywood films and a different dramatic œuvre, namely the Shakespearean romance. In *Pursuits of Happiness*, treating *A Midsummer Night's Dream* as an antecedent of George Cukor's PHILADELPHIA STORY, Cavell explains that he is not interested in providing solid evidence for a relation between these two texts. His interest, instead, "is one of discovering, given the thought of this relation, what the consequences of it might be." He goes

1 See Elisabeth Bronfen, *Liebestod und Femme fatale. Der Austausch sozialer Energien zwischen Oper, Literatur und Film*, Frankfurt am Main: S. Fischer Verlag, 2004.

on to explain: "This is a matter not so much of assigning significance to certain events of the drama as it is of isolating and relating the events for which significance needs to be assigned." In other words: rather than reducing the problems of the latter film to the earlier drama, his curiosity is drawn by the question of why the concerns of Shakespeare's romantic comedy have worked themselves out in their particular shape in the subsequent film, and this includes understanding "what these 'concerns' are and how to think about those 'shapes.'"[2]

For my own project of crossmapping, the alignment of texts belonging to different media (early modern drama or 19th-century opera and modern cinema respectively) is as much about the detected similarity, which calls forth the comparative reading in the first place, as an insistence on the differences to which mapping one text onto another draws our attention. In this sense I would reformulate (or augment) Cavell so as to underscore the notion of reversibility in the proposed conversation between drama, libretto, literature, and film. To understand what the concerns are that work themselves out in analogous shapings—thus my claim—also entails asking what is different about these shapings? When a subsequent text refigures an earlier one, at a different historical moment and in a different medium, at issue is not only what is retained but also what is left out, what is re-encoded, re-figured, and as such aesthetically transformed in the process of the remediation. My critical term "crossmapping" is thus also meant to draw attention to precisely those shapings that exceed or fall outside the aesthetic formulas that the texts to be brought into conversation share, and in doing so compel us to interrogate the consequences of these transformations. At the same time,

2 Stanley Cavell, *Pursuits of Happiness. The Hollywood Comedy of Remarriage,* Cambridge, MA: Harvard University Press, 1981, p. 145. See also Elisabeth Bronfen, *Stanley Cavell zur Einführung*, Hamburg: Junius Verlag, 2009.

by charting an association between two texts (or sets of texts), predicated on the similarity of shared concerns, the analysis underscores the fact that both are mediations, even if both the medium chosen (be it drama, opera, literature, or film) is different, as is the historical context from which these texts emerge and which they reflect. If, furthermore, in the process of crossmapping an earlier text comes to be revisited in relation to one that succeeds it, this brings into focus the fact that the proposed analytic mapping is both transmedial and trans historical. The juxtaposition follows what Mieke Bal calls preposterous history. The re-vision produced by mapping one text onto another neither collapses past and present, nor does it reify the past as an object that we can grasp in an unmediated manner. Rather, what she calls preposterous history entails a hermeneutic reversal, "which puts what came chronologically first ('pre') as an aftereffect behind ('post') its later recycling."[3]

Given that I understand crossmapping first and foremost as a hermeneutic practice, it is useful to bring into play an example of such hermeneutic juxtapositions. Early on in the third episode of David Simon's THE WIRE, a chess game takes place, which prompts me to read this early 21st-century TV novel in relation to Shakespeare's first tetralogy of English history plays, *Henry VI 1–3* and *Richard III*.[4] In this scene, D'Angelo, the nephew of one of the drug lords of the West Baltimore projects, explains to his fellow foot soldiers the rules of the chess game. They, in turn, immediately pick up on the way these are analogous to the rules of the drug war taking place between them, their competitors, and the police, and thus are as applicable to their everyday life as to the game. To illustrate the rigid hierarchy at issue in chess, D'Angelo explains that

3 Mieke Bal, *Quoting Caravaggio. Contemporary Art, Preposterous History*, Chicago: University of Chicago Press, 1999, p. 7.
4 See David Simon, THE WIRE, HBO 2002–08, season 1, episode 3.

everyone stays who he is except the pawns. If one of them actually makes it all the way to the side of the other player, he gets to become any piece he wants to be, including the all-powerful queen.

So the first crossmapping at issue in this scene is an intratextual one. The characters, along with the viewers, are meant to recognize in the rules of chess a description of the feudal system of the drug world that THE WIRE seeks to make visible. The chess game serves as the template for the codes regulating the network of power which this TV novel wants to draw our attention to by formulating and formalizing the rules that organize all possible moves in relation to situations. The dramaturgically implied juxtaposition underscores that in both games (chess and the drug wars), each figure has a clearly defined place and role within a strictly hierarchical order in which power is incessantly renegotiated by virtue of political acts. The moves individual players can make are highly codified and ritually predetermined.

D'Angelo's scene of instruction, however, also draws our attention to the one hope that those who start out as pawns can harbor. With a combination of luck and audacity, the pawn can bypass all the other ranks and immediately become royalty. The pawn may be the most endangered position, but it is also the figure that most visibly points to the fragility of royal legitimacy, and it is precisely this rule in chess that opens up, as my crossmapping proposes, a suggestive line of connection between Simon's TV novel and the Shakespearean history plays. In chess the pawn is the piece that stands in for the particular circumstance within the rules of the game that allows for a self-declared right to absolute power. Having arrived at the other end of the chess board, this figure can proclaim itself royal. This is indeed what happens when, in the course of the third season, the newcomer Marlo can step into the power vacuum produced when D'Angelo's uncle is once again sent to prison. While in Shakespeare's history plays such claims remain the prerogative

of members of the ruling class, in Richard III's usurpation of the throne we find a similarly audacious act of self-legitimation. So the hermeneutic wager at issue in this second, intermedial crossmapping, now of two sets of texts (a series of history plays and five seasons of a quality TV series), is the way both shape a civil war along the lines of a game in which the situation individual players find themselves in determines the moves open to them. In this case two mappings are being juxtaposed: Shakespeare's first tetralogy (*Henry VI 1–3* and *Richard III*) re-imagines the thirty-year battle between two branches of the royal house of Plantagenet as a visceral aristocratic war game, transforming England into the territory on which this battle is fought. David Simon's teleplay in turn recalls a "thirty years' war on drugs," with Baltimore the playing field for urban centers in early 21st-century capitalism.[5] As such, both the TV series (2002–08) and the series of history plays (premiered 1591–93) shape concerns regarding actual historical domestic strife—the English Wars of Roses, the American War on Drugs—as a theatricalized game, in which the shifts in political power are embodied by individual characters/actors playing through the schemes open to them.

Without going into a detailed discussion of these multiply tiered cognitive mappings, what I would like to underscore is that this juxtaposition of distinct shapings draws into focus the way a particular domestic strife is theatricalized so as to reflect on cultural anxieties and national identities. While Shakespeare's first tetralogy discusses the succession of the first Tudor monarch, who takes over the throne from the tyrant Richard III, in the context of an early modern political culture in which the killing of kings was nothing unusual, it is above all a reflection of the dominant ideology of his own time and the cultural anxieties surrounding the reign of Elizabeth I. If, in turn, Shakespeare's reshaping of the early English chronicles foregrounds the way power is seen "to depend not on legitimacy but on legitimation, on the capacity of the contender to seize and appropriate the signs of authority," this is precisely also what dramaturgically shapes Simon's concern with urban domestic warfare as a way of understanding the destructive aspects of both late capitalism and the war on drugs.[6] So my point is the following: the proposed crossmapping isolates a similar mode of re-imagining a particular political strife, albeit at different historical moments—early modern struggle over sovereignty, early 21st-century struggles over global capitalism—and in different media. My wager is that by looking at the Shakespearean dramas through the lens of their subsequent reshaping in

5 See David Simon, "Prologue", in Rafael Alvarez, *The Wire. The Truth be Told*, New York: Grove Press, 2009, p. 11.

6 See Graham Holderness, *Shakespeare's History Plays. Richard II to Henry V*, New Casebooks, London: Macmillan Palgrave, 1992, p. 12.

Simon's TV novel we see both in new light: we explore and explain one set of mappings (a chess game onto zones of the violence perpetrated by drug wars) with another (the war preceding Tudor ascendency onto the reign of its last representative, Elizabeth I).

The investigation into intermedial correspondences and connections proposed by crossmapping transcends the issue of acknowledged influence and explicit citation, even as it is underwritten by a double move. On the one hand I would claim that a later text (THE WIRE) maps certain constellations or concerns found in an earlier text (Shakespeare's first tetralogy) onto contemporary cultural and philosophical concerns. On the other, given the discernible analogies between both series of texts, it is equally fruitful to map onto Shakespeare's plays the way in which Simon's TV series responds to its own contemporary cultural crisis. Crossmapping, in other words, entails using historically later texts as the point of departure for a speculation on their cultural origin and, in so doing, looking—to stay with my example—at Shakespeare through the lens of his subsequent, albeit implicit, recyclings. Which is to say that the refiguration is performatively constructed by the proposed reading. Rather than simply proposing a relation of influence, crossmapping sheds light on neuralgic points that connect both cultural moments. The lines of connection opened allow us, for example, to read Shakespeare's plays as anticipating something that will come to be significant again at a different historical moment, albeit in a different guise. At the same time this hermeneutic strategy can also help us to discuss what Shakespeare can teach us about modernity. However, uncovering significant relationships between an earlier and a later text not only allows us to discover those passages for which our readings may offer fresh meaning. Equally productive is the way in which, having found and then charted certain correspondences, the one text shines through the other precisely because the mapping in fact produces no perfect fit.

As such, as a critical strategy, crossmapping is explicitly indebted to the cultural practice of cross-dressing, in which the gender assumed in masquerade never fully screens out the other gender. Asking about the manner in which Shakespeare anticipates thematic and rhetorical formalizations that will bear fruit *again* at a later date also means noticing seminal differences in the shapings offered by the early modern poet. I speak of *cross*mapping because my concern is a dialectically conceived intersection between two lines of thinking, understanding, and shaping of concerns. If, as my example suggests, a given oeuvre (Shakespeare's plays) has had a resilient afterlife, the question is also what shifts have occurred in the course of such cultural survival. In other words, crossmapping draws attention to the way difference nevertheless comes into play within the very survival of cultural energies that Shakespeare's texts have engendered over the ages. Indeed, the cross I am interested in involves a constant oscillation between past and present, between the prior text and its subsequent refiguration along the lines of what Roland Barthes has called the duplicity of the signifier. In his essay "Myth Today," Barthes includes a description of sitting in a car and looking at the scenery through the window. His point is that one can focus at will on the scenery or on the window, so as to grasp either the presence of the glass while the landscape is unfocussed and at a distance, or focus the gaze on the depth of the landscape and screen out the transparency of the glass. What one cannot do however, according to Barthes, is see both glass and landscape at the same time.[7]

Applied to the juxtaposition of texts at issue in crossmapping this means that, even as we focus on either the prior or the subsequent text we sense the presence of the other. Through our shifting focus, each is performatively enhanced by the

7 See Roland Barthes, "Myth Today" (1957), in *Mythologies*, New York: Hill and Wang, 1972, p. 123.

meanings discovered. While the lines of connection are given by the concerns and shapings shared by the texts brought into the conversation, the heuristic consequences are (as in cross-dressing) performative. The point of what I am calling a hermeneutic strategy is that it allows one to grasp a set of texts simultaneously, precisely because one is analytically compelled to move constantly backwards and forwards between them, without privileging the one over the other.

For this reason I have found myself compelled to rethink Walter Benjamin's notion of translatability. If, for him, translation is a form that circles an unfathomable, mysterious kernel, translatability must be inherent to the text, albeit not as its essence. It means, rather, "that a specific significance inherent in the original manifests itself in its translatability. [...] a translation issues from the original—not so much from its life as from its afterlife."[8] Indeed, as Benjamin goes on to note, it is in the process of being translated that the life of the original attains "its latest, continually renewed, and most complete unfolding" (p. 255). Afterlife implies transformation and renewal, implies that the original undergoes a change: there is "a maturing process" (p. 256). In its "preposterous" stance, crossmapping explores precisely this notion of survival (*Überleben*), afterlife (*Fortleben*), and maturation (*Nachreife*), not only in terms of the question of translatability from one language to another but also extending this to the kinship between different media (be these literary, dramatic or visual). Benjamin's argument is predicated on an idiosyncratic notion of aesthetic genealogy. The original that comes to be translated contains an intention (or what Cavell calls "concern") that can never be grasped directly but only *in* and *as* a translation. In addition to what can be refigured and reme-

8 Walter Benjamin, "The Task of the Translator," in *Selected Writings, Volume 1, 1913–1926*, ed. Marcus Bullock and Michael W. Jennings, Cambridge, MA: Harvard University Press, 1996, p. 254ff.

diated, there remains something that cannot be communicated (*ein Nicht-Mitteilbares*). Thus the articulation of difference (qua transformation) emerges as key in the visual analogy Benjamin offers: "Fragments of a vessel that are to be glued together must match one another in the smallest details, although they need not be like one another. In the same way a translation, instead of imitating the sense of the original, must lovingly and in detail incorporate the original's way of meaning, thus making both the original and the translation recognizable as fragments of a greater language, just as fragments are part of a vessel." (p. 260)

If Benjamin's emphasis on the translatability of ways of meaning (*Art des Meinens*) recalls what Cavell calls shapes, at issue for both is the cultural survival of something hidden and fragmentary that nevertheless resonates in subsequent re-articulations of earlier texts. To return to the notion of crossing as the articulation of an intersection, each subsequent formalization or shaping "touches the original", as Benjamin puts it, "lightly and only at the infinitely small point of the sense," so as to pursue its own course (p. 261). In that crossmapping retraces, indeed discovers, both this point of intersection and the diverging lines that emerge from it, the notion of cultural legacy it is engaged with also corresponds to the mappings of visual formulas (*Bildformeln*) and pathos formula (*Pathosformeln*) at the heart of Aby Warburg's *Mnemosyne Atlas*. Concerned with the duplicitous movement contained in the aesthetic formalization of transient but overwhelming emotions, Warburg notes, punning on the German word for griffin (*Vogelgreif*): "Under the darkly whizzing beating of the griffin's wings, suspended between apprehension (*Ergreifung*) and profound emotion (*Ergriffenheit*), we dream the concept of consciousness."[9] The

9 Quoted in Dorothée Bauerle, *Gespenstergeschichten für ganz Erwachsene. Ein Kommentar zu Aby Warburgs Bilderatlas Mnemosyne*, Münster: Lit Verlag, 1988, p. 13.

set of panels in his library, onto which he charted the cultural survival of the pathos formulas of antiquity, even while incessantly changing the arrangement of his mappings, had a particular goal. He wanted to offer a visual, embodied articulation of the way any experience of art involves a productive tension between a state of being overpowered by an aesthetic experience and the ability to intellectually grasp it (*Begreifen*). The initial intensity requires a form to become comprehensible; understanding occurs on the level of formalization.

But what that also means, to return to my earlier point about multiple intra- and intertextual mappings, is that any work whose pathos overtakes the viewer/reader even while containing this intensity (intention, concern) is itself an aesthetic formalization of an earlier experience of overpowering emotion. This formula has already captured pathos by transferring intensity into a formalized image. The concept, the pathos formula, strikes a balance between apprehending an ungraspable intensity and disclosing this to be the shaping of an intense emotion. Or put another way: the first emergence of a pathos formula (which in Benjamin's discussion of translatability functions as the original) is always an aesthetic formalization. What is reiterated in subsequent periods and different styles is the formula. Only because the emotional intensity has been given shape can it re-emerge at a later date, in a different historical context and a different medium. What is thus tracked on Warburg's panels, which assemble a panoply of different figurations into a mapped series, is not only the cultural survival and indeed maturing of this pathos, but also the fact that we can discern this afterlife by virtue of its serial re-articulation.

As Georges Didi-Huberman has insisted, the survival of pathos formula can be understood as a poignant example for cultural haunting. To map the emotional intensity embodied in the movement of an expressive gesture, he suggests, entails "a knowledge in extensions, in associative relationships, in ever renewed montages, and no longer knowledge in straight lines, in a confined corpus, in stabilized typologies."[10] To claim that, with any subsequent resuscitation, an image formula gives expression to the very emotional intensity that had initially come to be contained in it, presupposes an unconscious memory that keeps erupting. In that crossmapping tracks and charts the image formulas that re-emerge, these can be taken as evidence of the way we continue to be haunted by the past. My claim is that such survival of traces from the past through the incessant revival of past pathos formulas is best charted by articulating unconventional and unexpected correspondences, rather than the explicit citations and acknowledged influences at issue in the more conventional understanding of intertextuality. Indeed, what is at stake is a more transversal knowledge of the inexhaustible complexity of a history we feel compelled to revisit because it insists on being taken note of, over and over again. What I thus take from Didi-Huberman is the way a hermeneutic gesture of montage articulates a "desire to reconfigure memory by refusing to fix memories—images of the past—in an ordered, or worse, a definitive narrative."[11] At issue for me is the serial collection of connected image formula in a configuration that incessantly changes.

While my own work is limited to aesthetic crossmappings, my hope is that the strategy I am proposing might be useful for other types of comparative readings: looking at current political events and concerns in relation to the past they reiterate and respond to; thinking about the past—as a plural site when we bring different cultures into conversation with each other—in relation to the consequences events have had for the way we think about them and about our own situations. Reading the

10 See Georges Didi-Huberman, "Foreword", in Philippe-Alain Michaud, *Aby Warburg and the Image in Motion*, New York: Zone Books, 2007, p. 10.

11 See Georges Didi-Huberman, *Atlas: How to Carry the World on One's Back*, Karlsruhe: ZKM, 2011, p. 20.

present, in the sense of a panel containing series of different, conflicting, and even contradictory mappings of current concerns, in terms of and in conjunction with a past that in its own differentiated complexity we can grasp by virtue of what it continues to mean for us. Ultimately, crossmapping is concerned with the way we inherit and pass on these mediations of the world, with how we can return to this legacy and resignify it in the double sense of revision—seeing again and refiguring, revising, reconceiving it.

Christian Ritter

Transdisciplinarity—a Double-Agent Operation?

A Commentary on Elisabeth Bronfen's Crossmapping Concept

In 1995 the CIA Historical Review Program released a classified paper entitled *Observations on the Double Agent*. As a guideline for counter-intelligence activities, the 1962 document characterizes the reasons, models, and methods for running operations in the dim and dangerous field of espionage and intelligence. Even the text's introduction leaves no doubt that work with or as a double agent is necessarily filled with snares and pitfalls, and places special requirements both on professionals and methods: "Directing even one double agent is a time-consuming and tricky undertaking that should be attempted only by a service having both competence and sophistication."[1]

The same could be said of research in the uncertain territory of transdisciplinarity. Research that finds itself organized between the rationalities, sensitivities, and requirements of a number of disciplines is organizationally complex. It requires a high degree of reflection on methods and paradigms, as well as intense preoccupation with the habitual preferences and

1 F. M. Begoum, "Observations on the Double Agent" (1962), in *Studies in Intelligence*, 6/01 (1995), https://www.cia.gov/library/center-for-the-study-of-intelligence/kent-csi/vol6no1/html/v06i1a05p_0001.htm (accessed February 26, 2019).

individual expectations of each person involved. One could say that transdisciplinary research is a time-consuming and tricky undertaking that should be attempted only by scholars with both competence and sophistication.

Admittedly, the life-threatening hostility between different countries' intelligence services might be an inappropriate metaphor to describe the tension a researcher faces when he or she enters the academic culture's "in between." However, focusing on the double agent as a figure of thought with in-depth knowledge of two (or perhaps more) fields of activity helps to shift focus from transdisciplinarity as a principle of operation and organization to transdisciplinarity as a methodological paradigm and, moreover, to the researcher as an acting subject. This brings me back to Elisabeth Bronfen's *crossmapping*. In her paper, Bronfen presents crossmapping as a hermeneutic practice of analyzing the interplays between the aesthetics of multiple historical texts—in this case through comparative readings of Shakespeare's plays and David Simon's TV series THE WIRE (2002–08). Focusing on both literature and film, Bronfen's cultural analysis follows a substantial transdisciplinary approach that integrates thoughts and methods from different fields in the arts and humanities.

It thus becomes apparent that the productive linking of disciplines is not always dependent on team-based research, even though transdisciplinarity is often described as a cooperative practice in philosophy-of-science terms. At least in the humanities and social sciences it is not unusual for individual scholars to work with multiple perspectives and methods, and thus to move transversally through the canonical worlds of different disciplines. The same could be said of artists, whose work brings together methods and forms of knowledge from the discursive fields of art, the humanities, and science. This disciplinary "in between" or "this and that" is facilitated by a certain proximity between the disciplines involved, through shared themes and subjects, or through related methodological approaches.

Bronfen's linking of the approaches of literature and film is an example of this.

Of course, individual researchers are not hermits; they form their approaches and insights within networks and through interactions with other academic (and non-academic) actors. Nevertheless, the specific subjectivity of transdisciplinarity as a single academic work highlights epistemological potential that can only be achieved in precarious positions within the "trading zones" of the disciplines. Consider, for instance, the incomplete and unarticulated knowledge of individuals whose ephemeral and contradictory nature may be lost if it is solidified and formalized (too) early—and thus made more manageable for the purpose of intersubjective communication.

This problem not only affects research processes but also the presentation and representation of knowledge, which are obligatory elements at the end of every research project. The question which therefore arises is how knowledge gained in transdisciplinary research can be presented as adequate in terms of both the subject and methodology used—and thus with all of the vagueness and ambivalence characteristic of the modern-day cultural grammar. In 2013 Bronfen teamed up with Agnieszka Lulinska to test how the methodological linking of research and its presentation might look with the curation of the Kunsthalle Bonn's exhibition *Cleopatra: the Eternal Diva.*[2] Bronfen and Lulinska effectively transferred the comparative methodology of crossmapping to the spatial and material environment of the artistic space, so that intertextual and transmedia readings became subjectively comprehensible.

However, younger researchers, in particular, who are under pressure to achieve publication and legitimation, are hardly encouraged by the persistent conventions of the disciplines

2 See www.bundeskunsthalle.de/ausstellungen/kleopatra.html (2013; accessed February 26, 2019).

and funding agencies to experiment with (new) forms that carry connotations of being "un-academic." Such experimental (e.g. interactive, scenographic, or performative) formats are more likely to be found outside of the academic world or in addition to traditional formats like journals, chapters, or monographs. To avoid undermining their professional position, transdisciplinary researchers must behave like spies; if they do not wish to jeopardize their career, their working method must remain secret—and they must play their "role" as necessary in the respective context. Indeed, this is the only way they can successfully lay claim to integrity. It could therefore be concluded that transdisciplinary research is a privilege that has much to do with the institutional status of the scholars involved.

Concluding questions

Consideration of crossmapping as a transdisciplinary approach to cultural analysis raises two key questions. The first concerns transdisciplinary research as a methodological approach. The strength of a transdisciplinary practice driven by individual scholars lies in the fact that its epistemological potential is often strongly determined by subjective experiences and interests. Elisabeth Bronfen's crossmapping is one example of this. However, the subjective nature of the method requires intelligent reflection on the nature of one's own involvement. On the other hand, research undertaken by individual researchers favors forms of knowledge whose "obstinacy" (*Eigensinn*) threatens to be lost amid the translation and restructuring processes that are necessary for team-based research. The question is thus whether (and how) the concept of crossmapping can in any way also be a collaborative practice in which individuals from different disciplines can work together. In other words, is crossmapping a suitable method for integrating not only different disciplines but also different *subjective* viewpoints in a collective cultural analysis?

The second question deals with the aesthetic strategies through which the knowledge gleaned through transdisciplinary research can be presented—in such a way that the open, hybrid, and often contradictory nature of this methodological approach is not overshadowed by the dominant codes of disciplinary and institutional representation. Here the question which arises is whether or not we require an understanding of transdisciplinarity that also resolutely permits the representation of academic insights in "trans mode." This concerns both individual research and cooperatively organized research, and is ultimately a political question insofar as it triggers discussion of the paradigms of institutional recognition and funding.

In the world of intelligence, it would be a nightmare if a double agent felt equally beholden to different services. However, a less essentialist approach is required for scholarly work: academic quality should not be a question of loyalty to any one discipline.

Hans-Jörg Rheinberger

Away from the Disciplines[1]

The notion of two cultures in regard to the sciences and the humanities, and how to overcome the boundaries between the two realms of knowledge, has been a topic of debate for over half a century.[2] This is how the much-quoted but little-read Charles Percy Snow put it in 1959: "Literary intellectuals at one pole—at the other scientists, and as the most representative, the physical scientists. Between the two a gulf of mutual incomprehension—sometimes (particularly among the young) hostility and dislike, but most of all lack of understanding."[3] His essay concluded with a call to action: "Closing the gap between our cultures is a necessity in the most abstract intellectual sense, as well as in the most practical. When those two senses have grown apart, then no society is going to be able to think with wisdom."[4]

1 This article is based on and reproduces a part of Hans-Jörg Rheinberger, "Culture and Nature in the Prism of Knowledge," in *History of Humanities* 1 (2016), pp. 155–181.

2 The literature on this question is enormous. To name just a few works spanning the past three decades: Wolf Lepenies, *Between Literature and Science: The Rise of Sociology*, trans. R. J. Hollingdale, Cambridge: Cambridge University Press, 1988; Arkady Plotnitsky, *The Knowable and the Unknowable: Modern Science, Nonclassical Thought and the Two Cultures*, Ann Arbor: University of Michigan Press, 2002; Richard E. Lee and Immanuel Wallerstein, *Overcoming the Two Cultures: Science versus the Humanities in the Modern World-System*, London: Routledge, 2004; Jost Halfmann and Johannes Rohbeck (eds.), *Zwei Kulturen der Wissenschaft – revisited*, Weilerswist: Velbrück, 2007; Christine Charyton (ed.), *Creativity and Innovation among Science and Art. A Discussion of the Two Cultures*, Berlin, etc: Springer, 2015.

3 C. P. Snow, *The Two Cultures and the Scientific Revolution* (1959), New York: Cambridge University Press, 1969, p. 4.

4 Ibid., p. 50.

Snow's lament and his appeal for change followed on the heels of the Sputnik shock, at the peak of the Cold War, and his diagnosis was unmistakably that of a systemic deficit. The Western world was wasting a resource: "There seems then to be no place where the cultures meet. [...] At the heart of thought and creation we are letting some of our best chances go by default. The clashing point of two subjects, two disciplines, two cultures—of two galaxies, so far as that goes—ought to produce creative chances. In the history of mental activity that has been where some of the breakthroughs came. The chances are there now. But they are there, as it were, in a vacuum, because those in the two cultures can't talk to each other."[5]

Such was the perception of the context in which, half a century ago, the call for interdisciplinarity arose, and it has not dwindled since.[6] Clearly, this has been no transient fad. On the contrary, I believe it is symptomatic of a profound reconfiguration in the domain of the sciences and their evolution on both sides of the divide over the course of the twentieth century. Was the complaint of the physicist, writer, and politician C. P. Snow—himself highly skilled in moving between the cultures—a premonition that an epoch was ending, a classic owl of Minerva spreading its wings?

I would like to begin my remarks with a brief digression into the history of scientific disciplines. That very brevity means it will border on caricature, but I hope it will nevertheless serve to frame my argument. The disciplines as we know them from our university canon are not yet 200 years old. Even in the late

5 Ibid., p. 16.

6 For the early German context, see Helmut Holzhey (ed.), *Interdisziplinär*, Basel: Schwabe, 1974; for an even earlier example from France, see Louis Althusser, *Philosophy and the Spontaneous Philosophy of the Scientists (1967), & Other Essays*, trans. Warren Montag, London: Verso, 1990. The literature on interdisciplinarity, and subsequently also transdisciplinarity, has grown immensely and branched off into many different subject areas. This is not the place to review them.

eighteenth century, individuals approaching the unified competence of a scholar, *Gelehrter* or *savant*, were common. When the natural sciences began to take shape in the late seventeenth century and over the course of the eighteenth century, in part developing out of natural philosophy and in part emancipating themselves from medicine, they found their home in the philosophical faculties.[7] The authors of the French *Encyclopédie* were technicians, literary figures, naturalists, anthropologists, students of society, and philosophers—not only as a group, but often enough uniting those callings in various combinations within a single person. The Encylopédistes probably would not even have understood Snow's worries about the separation of cultures in the universe of knowledge as being a problem at all.

It was only in the course of the nineteenth century that this unified competence began to fragment, visibly and substantially. However, the perimeters dividing the subjects and disciplines that took shape in the universities over the nineteenth century were not imposed from outside; they sprang from powerful internal dynamics of differentiation, in particular within the natural sciences themselves. As early as 1862, Hermann Helmholtz, having moved from the University of Bonn to the University of Heidelberg in 1858, asked at his inauguration as prorector: "Who shall be able to overlook the whole? – who may hold in his hand the connecting thread, and find his way through the labyrinth? ... We are now inclined to smile on hearing, that in the seventeenth century Kepler was called to fill the post of Professor of Mathematics and Moral Philosophy at

7 Thus Germany's first chair of zoology was established in 1810 at the philosophical faculty of the newly founded University of Berlin. See Ilse Jahn, "Zur Herausbildung biologischer Disziplinen an der Berliner Universität im 19. Jahrhundert, mit besonderer Berücksichtigung der Zoologie," in Hubert Laitko and Regine Zott (eds.), *Zur Entwicklung der biologischen Disziplinen in Berlin, insbesondere an der Berliner Universität*, Berlin: Akademie der Wissenschaften der DDR, 1982, pp. 1–16.

Grätz."[8] Later in the lecture, he elaborated: "In this state of the case, when the main trunk of the sciences had spread out into an infinity of branches, – when marked contrasts have been developed between the different compartments, – when it is patent that no individual mind can hope to grasp the whole, or even any considerable portion of that whole – the question arises, is it any longer desirable to keep all the sciences together as it were under the same roof?"[9]

Helmholtz went on to ground his call for the university to be maintained with all its different subjects as a privileged site of mediation and understanding. He based this appeal on the need to preserve a "state of healthy equilibrium between the different faculties of the mind," especially between the humanities and the natural sciences, to which Helmholtz ascribed different but equally valid forms of induction: "logical" and "artistic" induction.[10] It is worth noting that although for the university context Helmholtz named the humanities as the site of a mode of thinking complementary to the natural sciences, it was in the arts that he saw this mode of thinking realized in its highest form. Here he doubtless had in mind the giant of intellectual life in Germany in the early nineteenth century, Johann Wolfgang von Goethe.

The process of gradual differentiation took hold not only in the natural sciences, but equally in the human sciences, which in addition were now separating out into humanities in the narrower sense and social sciences. At the height of this process, in the late nineteenth century, the humanities began to demarcate themselves more assertively vis-à-vis the natural sciences, whereas the social sciences started to emulate them.

8 Hermann Helmholtz, *On the Relation of the Natural Sciences to the Totality of the Sciences: An Address Delivered before the University of Heidelberg*, trans. C. H. Schaible, London: C. F. Hodgson, 1869, pp. 6–7.
9 Ibid., p. 10.
10 Ibid., pp. 10, 14.

Both moves were a reaction to the natural sciences' expanding validity claims and their contention to be the most efficacious, and thus foremost, fields of knowledge. Wilhelm Dilthey's distinction between the natural sciences' aspiration to *explain* the phenomena of nature and the cultural sciences' or humanities' aspiration to *understand* history,[11] along with Wilhelm Windelband's distinction between nomothetic and idiographic scholarship,[12] left deep marks in the academic consciousness of the fin de siècle. One substantial factor dignifying the humanities was the express declaration by leading natural scientists of the period—such as Emil Du Bois-Reymond in his famous and long-influential "Ignorabimus" address[13]—that it would forever be impossible to explain matters of consciousness by means of the natural sciences. Another was the gradual relativization of even the most fundamental concepts in the natural sciences as a result of the field's own inner expansions.

It is common knowledge that this process of schism, cementing a Cartesian dualism, as it were, and the codification of its methodological rationales left certain areas of knowledge—and not necessarily minor ones—for which the universal division into matter and mind, nature and culture, were problematic from the outset. This is true for the social sciences, which were beginning to take shape at the threshold of the nineteenth to the twentieth century, but it is especially true

11 Wilhelm Dilthey, *Selected Works*, vol. I, *Introduction to the Human Sciences* (1883), trans. Michael Neville, ed. Rudolf A. Makkreel and Frithjof Rodi, Princeton, NJ: Princeton University Press, 1989.

12 Wilhelm Windelband, *Geschichte und Naturwissenschaft*, Strassburg: Heitz, 1894.

13 Emil Du Bois-Reymond, "Über die Grenzen des Naturerkennens" (1872), in *Reden von Emil Du Bois-Reymond*, Leipzig: Veit & Co., 1912, vol. 1, pp. 441–473. For a recent study of the dispute around Du Bois-Reymond's "Ignorabimus" lecture, see Kurt Bayertz, Myriam Gerhard, and Walter Jaeschke (eds.), *Weltanschauung, Philosophie und Naturwissenschaft im 19. Jahrhundert*, vol. 3, *Der Ignorabimus-Streit*, Hamburg: Felix Meiner, 2007.

for the human sciences in the most literal sense of the word, the sciences of the human being and human faculties, such as anthropology, archaeology, linguistics, and psychology.[14] Evidently, if we accept the bisection presented above, the objects of these disciplines must be regarded as hybrid, ambivalent things. They could not, and still cannot, be fully attributed to one domain or the other—or not without losing precisely their most interesting qualities, the essential properties that drive their inquiry. This means, however, that even during the heyday of academic differentiation into ontologically grounded disciplines, a large section of scholarly investigation was located in a space that spanned the rift between the two sides or, one might also say, filled in that very rift without making the difficulties of attribution any easier to resolve.

Let us look more closely for a moment at the natural sciences half of the equation. In deliberations of this kind, they are usually depicted as a compact and monolithic "side," with sharply delineated contours that seem to be set down once and for all. But is this actually the case? Take biology as an example. It was only during the first half of the nineteenth century that biology began to acquire a profile of its own, establishing comparatively clear borders against physics and chemistry. From the beginning of the century, it had centered on botany and zoology, which now increasingly fanned out into taxonomy on the one hand, morphology and anatomy on the other. Around the mid-century, those subjects clustered under an overarching theory of the development of life on earth: evolutionary theory. Also in the middle of the nineteenth century, physiology consolidated itself. It seceded from anatomy and increasingly relied on the cell theory, as a science of the general phenomena of life common to both animals and plants—such was the for-

14 Still very much worth reading on this matter is Edgar Morin, *Le paradigme perdu: La nature humaine*, Paris: Éditions du Seuil, 1973.

mulation chosen by the French physiologist Claude Bernard for the title of his last book.[15] Building on physiology and morphology, toward the end of the century experimental developmental biology began to gain substance. The start of the twentieth century was marked by the meteoric rise of a latecomer to the band of diversifying biological disciplines, genetics.[16] Physiology, developmental biology, and genetics together formed the core of a new experimental biology around the turn of the century, but each had constructed its own, mutually irreducible arsenal of methods. Referred to in the usage of the day as "general biology,"[17] they supplied the experimental counterweight to evolutionary biology with its predication on natural history.[18]

Between 1800 and 1900, then, the macroclimate of biology changed dramatically. Around 1800, the term "biology" had been introduced to articulate the aspiration that research into the particularities of life was to acquire a status of its own, to delimit life from its physical surroundings as a phenomenon *sui generis*.[19] In his reflections on the study of organic life, Immanuel Kant had ultimately remained undecided whether or not it was in principle possible to subjugate that study to the

15 Claude Bernard, *Lectures on the Phenomena of Life Common to Animals and Plants (1878–79)*, trans. Hebbel E. Hoff, Roger Guillemin, and Lucienne Guillemin, Springfield, IL: Charles C. Thomas, 1974.

16 For a detailed account, see Staffan Müller-Wille and Hans-Jörg Rheinberger, *A Cultural History of Heredity*, Chicago: The University of Chicago Press, 2012.

17 See Manfred D. Laubichler and Michael Hagner (eds.), *Der Hochsitz des Wissens. Das Allgemeine als wissenschaftlicher Wert*, Zurich: diaphanes, 2006.

18 On this point, Ernst Mayr's study remains unsurpassed: Ernst Mayr, *The Growth of Biological Thought: Diversity, Evolution, and Inheritance*, Cambridge, MA: Harvard University Press, 1982.

19 See, for example, Torsten Kanz, "'... die Biologie als die Krone oder der höchste Strebepunct aller Wissenschaften.' Zur Rezeption des Biologiebegriffs in der romantischen Naturforschung (Lorenz Oken, Ernst Bartels, Carl Gustav Carus)," *NTM* 15 (2006), pp. 77–92.

mechanical paradigm of the contemporary sciences.[20] Although most biologists of the time assumed the existence of a *nisus formativus* or formative drive of some sort, its portrayal remained ambivalent, wavering between Newtonianism with a biological turn and less rigorous vitalist approaches. In the course of the nineteenth century, the mechanical paradigm gained the upper hand, especially in physiology. By 1900, and in contrast to a century before, "general biology" designated the endeavor to identify the structures and functions shared by all living beings, in other words to define them from the inside out as living systems. In turn this meant that the fundamental question of life was now posed in terms of system and the peculiarities of living systems. This history has usually been written as the history of a battle between materialism and vitalism, an approach that has ultimately occluded rather than illuminated the real dynamics at stake. Incidentally, a lateral glance at the formation of the humanities across the nineteenth century suggests that the historiography of *their* real dynamics, too, suffers even today from a tendency to subsume their differentiation under the parallel dispute between materialism and idealism.

As the twentieth century progressed, the richly but more or less manageably differentiated disciplinary landscape within the life sciences experienced further profound change. At first it was two hybrid sciences that recharted the terrain and unsettled biology's boundary line against chemistry and physics, the frontier that biology had so painstakingly constructed at the beginning of the nineteenth century and that had already been disrupted once before, during the rise of physiology half a century later. One of those hybrid sciences was biochemistry, the other was biophysics. Both constructs were fusions that over-

20 For a trenchant commentary, see Peter McLaughlin, *Kant's Critique of Teleology in Biological Explanation*, Lewiston, NY: Edwin Mellen Press, 1990.

came a fundamental distinction in the natural sciences, while also becoming largely independent disciplines of their own. Around the middle of the twentieth century, finally, a formation arose that has come to be known as molecular biology. Again, it appeared as a multiple hybrid, amalgamating biophysical and biochemical techniques with the questions and methodologies of genetics. Molecular biology—and its core, molecular genetics—reinstated the link between physics, chemistry, and biology, but in a new form. The configuration gave rise to an entirely novel notion of the particularity of life, of biological specificity. It revolved around the concepts of genetic "information" and genetic "program," and it used a language that absorbed elements from all its parent domains.[21] Reproduction, development, and self-preservation—Kant's three specific properties of organic life—came together in a unified paradigm that additionally adopted the vocabulary of the systems science predominant at the time, cybernetics. It not only materially located these properties in biological macromolecules but also, with the concept of information, stamped those molecules with an element of the irreducibly formal.[22] In the framework of morphology, since Goethe's day the notion of form had marked an interface between biology and the humanities; this interface now seemed to be located in the molecules themselves. The conjunction was properly noted at the time by at least some of the actors.[23]

21 The classic account is François Jacob, *The Logic of Life: A History of Heredity* (1970), trans. Betty E. Spillmann, New York: Vintage, 1976; see also Christina Brandt, *Metapher und Experiment. Von der Virusforschung zum genetischen Code*, Göttingen: Wallstein, 2004; with specific reference to Jacob also Hans-Jörg Rheinberger, *An Epistemology of the Concrete: Twentieth-Century Histories of Life*, Durham, NC: Duke University Press, 2010, chap. 10.

22 See Lily E. Kay, *Who Wrote the Book of Life? A History of the Genetic Code*, Stanford, CA: Stanford University Press, 2000.

23 See especially François Jacob, Philippe L'Héritier, Roman Jakobson, and Claude Lévi-Strauss, "Vivre et parler," in *Les Lettres Françaises* 1221

Molecular biology soon attained the status of a basic science within biology, but it was not to enjoy its disciplinary integrity for long.[24] Itself the outcome of a prodigious disciplinary hybridization, it burst its own disciplinary banks just as prodigiously. The new biology was initially restricted to the basic analysis of molecular structures and processes, but in the 1970s it opened up the way for a new genetic technology in multifarious guises, all of them based on macromolecules as tools to work on cells. As a toolkit, it spread throughout the life sciences, agriculture, and medicine. The human genome project was the epistemic articulation of this new formation; its economic articulation was the rise of the molecular biotechnology industry with close ties between start-ups and university research. I have discussed this point elsewhere in more detail.[25]

At present what is being called synthetic biology is increasingly gaining ground within this biological and technological complex. Synthetic biology comes laden with the hitherto unresolved social, cultural, and ethical questions raised by applications of genetic technology and reproductive biology in medicine, human reproduction, and the bio-industry.[26] In these areas, the objects of research—which are simultaneously prospective objects of application—are generally no longer determined by their natural (physical, chemical, biological) or technical aspects alone; they too are multiply hybrid objects

(February 14 and 21, 1968), pp. 3–7; François Jacob, "Le modèle linguistique en biologie," in *Critique* 322 (1974), pp. 197–205.

24 See Soraya de Chadarevian and Hans-Jörg Rheinberger (eds.), "Disciplinary Histories and the History of Disciplines: The Challenge of Molecular Biology," in *Studies in History and Philosophy of Biological and Biomedical Sciences* 40, special issue (2009).

25 See Staffan Müller-Wille and Hans-Jörg Rheinberger, *Das Gen im Zeitalter der Postgenomik. Eine wissenschaftshistorische Bestandsaufnahme*, Frankfurt am Main: Suhrkamp, 2009.

26 See, for example, Bernadette Bensaude-Vincent and Dorothée Benoit-Browaeys, *Fabriquer la vie. Où va la biologie de synthèse?* Paris: Seuil, 2011.

that inextricably imbricate aspects of both nature and culture and cannot be handled responsibly if that imbrication is disregarded. Technological and cultural potential decides what attains epistemic relevance, and epistemic potential decides what can attain technological-cultural relevance. This brings us to a configuration of the relationship between nature and culture that not only invites but challenges us to turn our attention to the two categories of nature and culture themselves, to contemplate their emergence and their historically changing relationships. As Bruno Latour puts it, inverting the image of the Gordian knot: "For twenty years or so, my friends and I have been studying these strange situations that the intellectual culture in which we live does not know how to categorize. [...] Whatever label we use, we are always attempting to retie the Gordian knot by crisscrossing, as often as we have to, the divide that separates exact knowledge and the exercise of power—let us say nature and culture."[27]

Let me briefly summarize what I have argued for so far. Firstly, even at the high-water marks of the separation between the natural sciences and the humanities there have always been hybrid research fields and objects that nestled between the stipulated "two cultures." Secondly, it was the dynamics of historical development *inside* the sciences that first introduced, then hardened, increasing disciplinary separations in the nineteenth century; in the course of the twentieth century those dynamics created a certain counter-movement, with extensive cross-reactions and blurring of disciplinary boundaries. Thirdly, researchers today—also in many areas of the natural sciences and especially technology—are not only obliged to move within new partitions that no longer coincide with the knowledge boundaries of the traditional subjects, but also find a cultural dimension

27 Bruno Latour, *We Have Never Been Modern*, trans. Catherine Porter, Cambridge, MA: Harvard University Press, 1993, p. 3.

entering their knowledge objects, to such an extent that it cannot be ignored in their definitions without forfeiting meaning.

In the foregoing I have deliberately focused on the natural sciences because it is there that distinctions and boundaries—especially by inhabitants of the camp of the humanities—are commonly assumed to be given and beyond question. In fact, as even this superficial sketch of the development of biology over the past two centuries has shown, the natural sciences are exposed to inexorable historical dynamism. Of course subjects in the humanities and cultural or social sciences are just as malleable, but—within the natural sciences camp—that very fact is often regarded as one of their disqualifying features. One further point becomes significant for the extent to which the border zones of the two large-scale formations have begun to shift: the observation of an emerging symmetry. According to the ETH physicist Martin Quack, "border crossings in *both* directions" are on the agenda today.[28]

It seems to me that for both sides, the natural sciences and the humanities, it is becoming increasingly important to develop an awareness of the dynamics of change in the research *objects* specific to each. Like the applications of knowledge, the objects of knowledge all have their historical trajectories, which depend importantly upon the instrumental options for accessing them in the first place and shaping them accordingly. The importance of these options of access is the reason why I prefer to keep to the term historical epistemology here, as opposed to historical ontology.[29] The resulting histories are sometimes ramified and recalcitrant; their life spans differ and so does

28 Martin Quack, "Naturwissenschaften! Warum überhaupt? Warum nicht?" in *Gegenworte. Hefte über den Disput über Wissen* 26 (2011), p. 32.

29 Hans-Jörg Rheinberger, "Introduction," in *On Historicizing Epistemology: An Essay*, trans. David Fernbach, Stanford, CA: Stanford University Press, 2010; see also Ian Hacking, *Historical Ontology*, Cambridge, MA: Harvard University Press, 2004.

their impact, and occasionally the objects of epistemic interest accompanying them may fade back into obscurity and become marginalized.[30] After all, the historical development of disciplines that I have highlighted is itself nothing more than the organizational and institutional expression of the underlying dynamics of knowledge objects. It is therefore vital to attend to the historicity—and thus the cultural, technological, and social mediatedness—of the *things* that populate our scientific and scholarly world, and not only that of theories and concepts or abstract methodological principles such as understanding and explanation or equivalent general distinctions. If I am right, the view of the sciences that focuses on the history of ideas and shuns anything concrete or practical has contributed to an image of science as cleansed of culture, something long propagated by the sciences themselves. This is where we find the genuine task of the history of science, as a representative of which I am addressing this issue. To put it in a nutshell: The task is to examine *all* the sciences, including the natural sciences, as cultural techniques.[31]

In the current battles over the proper understanding of science, this terminological choice conveys something of the effort involved in and the attempt to avoid locating the sciences, and knowledge of nature accordingly, simply on the side of nature. Of course this still happens often enough even today in certain expert discourses, but the positions I refer to here seek to characterize the natural sciences and scientific knowledge of nature as themselves deeply cultural phenomena, set about with historical conditions, and thereby to draw them a little way onto

30 Lorraine Daston (ed.), *Biographies of Scientific Objects*, Chicago: University of Chicago Press, 2000.

31 On the concept of cultural techniques, see Bernhard Siegert, *Cultural Techniques: Grids, Filters, Doors, and Other Articulations of the Real*, trans. Geoffrey Winthrop-Young, New York: Fordham University Press, 2015.

the side where the humanities have always been at home. One might consider this a necessary prerequisite for creating something like a vision of the unity of the sciences in all their irreducible plurality.

Hartmut von Sass

The Way of Science, or Away from Science

A Reply to Hans-Jörg Rheinberger

The title under which Hans-Jörg Rheinberger's considerations are summarized remains ambiguous. And I am not sure whether this ambivalence is really intended by the author. Is it about the way and development the scientific disciplines have so far covered historically—*the way of the disciplines*? Or are we dealing here with the invocation to finally disengage from the discipline of the disciplines—*away from (or even: away with) the disciplines*? Perhaps this does not represent a substantial alternative, some may argue, because the way of the disciplines might be a way that already leads away from the disciplines somewhere else. And yet, nevertheless, in the title's ambiguity also lies an ambiguity regarding the initial claim. While the way covered by science is one that is describable within a history of the sciences, the second reading seems to entail an appeal to act beyond disciplinarity in the time to come.

Rheinberger's text consists largely of an outline of the modern Western history of science, of a sketch that is itself an example of what the author calls "historical epistemology" (in slight contrast to Ian Hacking's "historical ontology").[1] In this

1 See Hans-Jörg Rheinberger, *Historische Epistemologie zur Einführung*, Hamburg: Junius, 2007; Ian Hacking, *Historical Ontology*, Cambridge, MA: Harvard University Press, 2004.

approach one exercises a particularly diachronically sensitive appreciation of science as a "cultural technique" and the genesis of its changeable objects. It is this appreciation that puts the stress on the descriptive version of the title: the way that the sciences have gone so far, and this is historically comprehensible. Contrary to this, the second version suggests that the title (and, hence, the entire text) should be read in an imperative way: the factual development of the disciplines as justification to leave the disciplines behind.

This history, recapitulated by Rheinberger, consists of the following chapters: He reminds us, first, that science's disciplinary structure did not emerge earlier than around 1800, thus during the educational politics of the late Enlightenment movement. The institution of the polymath becomes, second, an end-of-range model—disregarding a few romantic nerds—to be substituted by increasingly specialized experts responsible only for a particular discipline. From here a constellation arises that previously existed only rudimentarily, namely a culture of two cultures, or in Bruno Latour's phrasing, of "two chambers."[2] Nevertheless, third, this duality between (natural) sciences and humanities remains insufficient, wherefore we observe an internal differentiation during the 19th century, a differentiation that, Rheinberger holds, fully corresponds to the logic of the institutionally established subjects. Fourth, but much later, this two-chamber duality gets challenged by the social sciences that buck the simple allocation to either natural sciences or humanities. However, even this threefold classification is governed by the idea of having particular academic branches that are, finally, partially substituted by inter- and later transdisciplinary arrangements. Accordingly, cooperations between the disciplines emerge everywhere (*interdisciplinary correction*),

2 Bruno Latour, *We Have Never Been Modern*, trans. Catherine Porter, Cambridge, MA: Harvard University Press, 1993, esp. ch. 4.

and new subjects are formed and established beyond the ordinary disciplinary borders. They may be called hybrid for two reasons: they combine two or three formerly separated disciplines, a process that can be studied, for instance, in the rise of biochemistry, and they exceed the purely scientific framework, shown by using the example of molecular biology, a fairly new subject that brings together social and economic implications and undermines the allegedly strict separation between nature and culture (*transdisciplinary correction*).

Rheinberger critically summarizes this sketch by three key points: on the one hand, he holds that there have always been hybrid fields of research; hence figures like Leibniz, Goethe or Thomas Hobbes were forerunners of what we today are regaining institutionally in science, and resemble transdisciplinary scholars *avant la lettre*. On the other hand the sketched history of science does not reveal a linear development, but the very late rise of separated subjects linked with the liquefaction of the disciplinary limits once set. And finally the author highlights the cultural dimension informing our forms of knowledge in order to wake up from the dream of having pure knowledge and culturally purified insight.

Despite a great deal of agreement, there is now a greater deal of perplexity. The obvious difficulties connected with "historical epistemology" and what is described by that program are alluded to, but the reader remains alone with these difficulties. There are essentially three problems I would like to address briefly:

The problem of naturalization: Rheinberger's text begins with a reminder of the two cultures, the one of nature and its counterpart in the humanities or in arts. With and at the same time without Bruno Latour, the author underlines that knowledge is always *our* apparatus-*mediated* knowledge. Therefore, it is said, a strict division between nature and culture is obsolete, because knowledge does not belong solely on nature's side. However, Rheinberger does not push his case so far as Latour did in the late 1970s, namely that nature itself turns out to be an actor (or "actant") or that nature is, as it were, forming (the) culture. So the notion that knowledge does not exclusively belong to nature's camp, but rather and to an essential extent derives from our grasp of nature, sticks to the traditional line of epistemology insofar as it pays attention to the creative aspects of our approach to objects and things.[3]

I do not know many authors who would like to challenge this view. But it is one that should also be applied to historical epistemology itself. This program entails a claim about the dynamics of sciences, and insofar as historical epistemology is part of science, it talks about itself too. The naturalization of knowledge is tantamount to distributing knowledge to both sides or chambers: to nature and culture in their inseparability. Science, however, was presented by Rheinberger as "cultural technique" (without natural traits). So does not the application of the claim about historical epistemology to itself refute the thesis nature and culture cannot be separated? Since historical epistemology refers only to a cultural phenomenon, i.e. science and humanities, it therefore does not repudiate, but presupposes the (at least partial or heuristic) division between natural facts and cultural techniques.

Realism of institutions: If I understand correctly, the non-linear dynamics of sciences represents—up to its contemporary inter- and transdisciplinary architecture—a development that originates in the sciences themselves. Hence this dynamic is considered to be an intrinsically necessary phenomenon. Toward the end it is said accordingly:

3 See also Hans-Jörg Rheinberger, "Experimentalsysteme: Differenz, Graphematizität, Konjunktur," in his *Experiment – Differenz – Schrift. Zur Geschichte epistemischer Dinge*, Marburg: Basilisken-Presse, 1992, pp. 21–46, esp. 24–25.

> After all, the historical development of disciplines that I have highlighted is itself nothing more than the organizational and institutional expression of the underlying dynamics of knowledge objects.

The weight of that statement depends obviously on the meaning of "object" here. However, the general tone—despite other, more constructivist voices in the text—is in this passage a surprisingly realistic one: the occurrence of transdisciplinary research resembled a procedure that was demanded by science itself, and exclusively so.

This claim not only appears to be false, because it neglects all political, that is, ideological and generally non-scientific, aspects of forming science—or speaking with Ludwik Fleck, "the genesis and development of a scientific fact"[4]; it also does not provide what Rheinberger himself explicitly values, namely an underlining of the historical and cultural embeddedness of science and knowledge. How can it be that the institutionalization of science is supposed to be exclusively determined by its subject matter?

The future of disciplinarity: If one disregards the fact that the jargon of transdisciplinarity has already been promoted (or degraded) to the well-established arsenal of proposal prose, one might ask—contrary to the initial plausibility—what will become of the genuinely *disciplinary* tailoring of our universities in research and teaching? What does the future of disciplinarity look like, when the present time is progammatically dominated by transdisciplinarity?[5] We are told that the borders between the natural sciences and humanities should be mutu-

4 See Ludwik Fleck, *The Genesis and Development of a Scientific Fact*, ed. T. J. Trenn and R. K. Merton, with a foreword by Thomas Kuhn, Chicago: University of Chicago Press, 1979.

5 See Hans-Jörg Rheinberger, "Zur Historizität wissenschaftlichen Wissen: Ludwik Fleck, Edmund Husserl," in his *Epistemologie des Konkreten. Studien zur Geschichte der modernen Biologie*, Frankfurt am Main: Suhrkamp, 2006, pp. 21–36, esp. 25–26.

ally transgressed—but why? Furthermore, as stated at the end, one should stick to the idea of a unity of the sciences—but why? Finally, and returning to the beginning, who is really speaking here? Who is making these pleas? The historian of science, the historically-oriented epistemologist? But then the initially descriptive endeavor turns latently or suddenly into a normative gesture. And the "way of science" not only leads away from the disciplines but amounts to a call for exodus. Is the historiography not confounded with politics and matters of organization?

Yes, perhaps, it is, but that does not have to be a bad thing. It might only mean that historically-oriented science research has to work in a transdisciplinary manner as well. The oscillation between descriptive intention and normative endeavor should not be regretted. It might instead be a happy indication that Rheinberger himself is doing exactly what he is writing about: getting on the "way of sciences" to the beyond of scientific discipline and institutionalized disciplinarity.

Contributors

Harald Atmanspacher. Dr. habil., physicist and member of the executive board at the Collegium Helveticum, responsible for the natural sciences and engineering.

Andrea B. Braidt. Ph.D, researcher in comparative literature, film and cultural studies, vice-rector for art | research at the Academy of Fine Arts, Vienna.

Elisabeth Bronfen. Professor of English and American studies at the University of Zurich, global distinguished professor at New York University.

Florian Dombois. Artist and professor at the Institute for Art Education, Zurich University of the Arts.

Sabine Maasen. Friedrich Schiedel professor of sociology of science at the Technical University in Munich.

Marco Meier. Journalist and writer, Lucerne.

Jürgen Mittelstrass. Prof. em. of theoretical philosophy and philosophy of science at the University of Konstanz, Germany.

Hans-Jörg Rheinberger. Professor em. of molecular biology and history of science, former director of the Max Planck Institute for the History of Science in Berlin.

Christian Ritter. Ph.D, arts and media scholar and member of the executive board at the Collegium Helveticum, responsible for the art/media/design research area.

Hartmut von Sass. Associate professor of systematic theology and philosophy of religion at the University of Zurich and vice-director of the Collegium Helveticum.

Christoph Schenker. Professor at the Institute for Contemporary Art Research, Zurich University of the Arts.

Amrei Wittwer. Ph.D, pharmacologist and pain researcher, Bludenz, Austria.

First edition
ISBN 978-3-0358-0174-3

Layout: 2edit, Zurich
Printed in Germany

www.diaphanes.com